PROPHET
MUHAMMAD

The Seal of All Prophets

D1520175

PROPHET MUHAMMAD

The Seal of All Prophets

Rahime Kaya

TUGHRA BOOKS

New Jersey

Contents

Abdul Muttalib's Dream

"Sacrifice for your Lord, fulfill your vow!"

Upon hearing these words in his dream, Abdul Muttalib sacrificed a beautiful ram and distributed its meat to the needy people first thing in the morning. When night fell and he went to sleep, he heard the same voice in his dream, "Offer your Lord a bigger and better sacrifice!"

Under the influence of the dream, as soon as he woke up in the morning, he sacrificed beautiful cattle and distributed it amongst the poor. However, the same day that he sacrificed the cattle, he heard the same voice in his dream.

In the morning, he sacrificed a beautiful camel, and once again, distributed its meat to the needy. But the same voice was heard again that night, "Offer a bigger sacrifice to your Lord!"

This time around, Abdul Muttalib questioned the voice: "What is the bigger sacrifice?"

He was then told, "Remember your vow that you made to Allah many years ago. You asked Allah for a son. Your wish was fulfilled. Now fulfill your vow."

After hearing those words in his dream, Abdul Muttalib woke up drenched in sweat. His mind ventured off to the previous years of his life. Time had passed so quickly. Years before, he had another interesting dream, similar to this one. In his dream, the place of the Zamzam well was revealed to him. So with his only son, Harith, he went to the determined place and began to dig in search of the Zamzam well. The elders of Mecca also wanted to participate, and began digging with them. Over the course of history, the Zamzam well that Abraham's wife Hagar found was lost. When the people of Mecca made a big circle around Abdul Muttalib and said, "This is a legacy of our ancestor, Prophet Abraham's son, Ishmael," Abdul Muttalib responded to the crowd standing over him, "Allah appointed me to this task. He said, I should not allow you all to partner up."

In return they said, "Besides your only son, who else do you have to help you and protect you? You should not oppose us in this matter." They threatened him, saying, "By Allah, if we fight we will flog you."

Abdul Muttalib responded, "You are blaming me for not having many children. I swear to Allah, one day, if I have ten sons and they grow up to protect me, I will sacrifice one of them in the Ka'ba."

Afterwards, he continued to dig the well with his son Harith. Upon seeing Abdul Muttalib's determined behavior, the people of Mecca understood that they could not take part in finding Zamzam water, and just anxiously waited for the result. At the end of the third day, the walls of the well were reached and Abdul Muttalib showed his joy with exaltation. Afterwards, he continued digging, revealed the water source, and offered it for usage of all human beings, animals, and the whole existence. This case increased the dignity of Abdul Muttalib, a mighty leader whom the people of Mecca appointed for their affairs. In the meantime many years passed and Abdul Muttalib became a father of ten sons. Now through another dream, he has been reminded of his promise in return for his ten sons.

Prophet Muhammad: The Seal of All Prophets

The Day of Drawing Lots

L ittle by little, it began to dawn, and Mecca began to fill with the sun's sweet glow. For Abdul Muttalib, one of the most difficult days of his life was about to begin. Under the influence of his night dreams, he was thinking of his boys since he woke up. He was thinking about the world's most beautiful Abdullah. Unlike his brothers, a light shone out of Abdullah's forehead. Thanks to that light, his beauty became the talk of legends. The light on Abdullah's forehead had before shone on his father Abdul Muttalib's forehead; even before him, it had shone on his grandfather Hashim's forehead. This light that belonged to the Last Prophet came from the first created man and first Prophet, Adam, peace be upon him, all the way down to Prophet Abraham, peace be upon him, and the most honored of mankind. From Prophet Abraham, peace be upon him, it was transferred to his son Ishmael, peace be upon him, and was passed on from son to son until it reached Abdullah. Very little time was left to reach the original owner of this light that was created way before Adam's time as well.

When the sun had risen, everybody in Abdul Muttalib's house woke up. The sad father called his sons to his presence; told them about his story of digging the Zamzam and about his vow that he had made to Allah. He was unable to raise his head and spare any of them. After he pulled himself together, he told his children, "Now tell me, what do you think about it all?"

The children agreed on the same answer and said, "O father! If you made such a vow to Allah, you should definitely fulfill it. Whoever you choose from amongst us, we will surely obey you."

Upon hearing this, Abdul Muttalib said, "Well then, each of you grab an arrow and write your name on it. We will then go to the Ka'ba and let the officer cast the lots."

He had murmured and slurred his last words. Abdul Muttalib was going through a severe trial. He felt grief like a storm breaking inside him, but he was holding back his feelings. Under his breath, he was constantly repeating, "There is nothing to add to the vow made to Allah. I have to fulfill my vow." While he was walking towards the Ka'ba with his ten sons behind him, his inner judgment continued in the same manner.

They arrived at the Ka'ba, the first building and the first sanctuary built for Allah. There, Abdul Muttalib explained to the officer the reason for their visit. Having heard that he was going to sacrifice one of his sons upon casting the lot, the officer was astonished. Abdul Muttalib, the leader of Quraysh, handed over the arrows, and with a lush sound, he said, "Draw the lot."

If the officer had not known Abdul Muttalib, he would have tried to deter him from this act. However, there stood the most serious and respected man of Mecca. After looking at the arrows that were handed to him, he picked one of them. He read aloud the name written on the arrow, Abdullah.

Abdul Muttalib's heart burnt. Abdullah was his most beloved son. Nonetheless, he made a covenant with Allah, and thus, the provision was certain and could not be changed.

Holding Abdullah's hand, with the knife in his hand Abdul Muttalib walked toward the place where Abdullah was going to be sacrificed. Regarding the fulfillment of his vow, Abdul Muttalib acted obediently, and his son Abdullah surrendered to his judgment. The leaders of Quraysh who were witnesses, approached Abdul Muttalib immediately and said, "What are you trying to do O Abdul Muttalib?"

Abdul Muttalib, with a sad yet determined voice said, "I am going to sacrifice him."

They intervened, "Do not do this! You are respected among us. Today, if you sacrifice your child here, you will start a bad tradition. After this, everyone will start sacrificing their children."

But the whole conversation did not provide any solution to the fulfillment of the vow. Abdul Muttalib was not convinced. At that moment, a voice was raised from the crowd, "Do not do this! If you please, you may take him to Hijaz and tell the famous wise man about the situation. If he says, 'Sacrifice him,' then do it, but if he shows you another way, you do what you are told. This way, you will have kept your promise."

Abdul Muttalib found this suggestion quite reasonable. He put the knife in his hand aside, and with a group of people, he went to the wise man. First, he told him everything in detail. Then he asked the wise man to find a solution for them.

The wise man asked, "How much is the blood money in your society?"

"Ten camels," they responded.

He said, "So go back to your country and put forth the person meant for sacrifice and the ten camels. Afterwards, draw lots for both of them. If the man is picked, multiply the number of the camels by ten until the camels are picked. Once the camels are picked, you will have saved your man from sacrifice."

He was very pleased with this beautiful offer. Not wanting to waste time, they started their journey back to Mecca. Before carrying out the advice of the wise man, Abdul Muttalib turned to Allah and supplicated that this act result in an auspicious way. After that, they prepared the ten camels and started drawing lots. Abdul Muttalib withdrew to a corner and began praying to Allah with his most sincere feelings.

Abdullah's name was drawn first. By adding ten more camels, they repeated the process. It was again Abdullah's name that was drawn. Every time they added ten more camels and repeated the act nine times, and the arrows pointed to Abdullah. Finally ten more camels were added and only when the total number of camels reached a hundred, the drawing resulted with the camels. Everybody was very happy. They turned to Abdul Muttalib and said, "Surely, now Allah will be pleased with you."

But in order to be certain, the leader of Quraysh carried this process out three more times. Every time the arrow pointed towards the camels. Now, Abdul Muttalib's heart was satisfied and Abdullah was saved from being sacrificed in return for one hundred camels. Finally they sacrificed the hundred camels and distributed their meat to the needy. This way, Abdul Muttalib fulfilled his promise to Allah with a sincere heart.

Blessed Marriage

At the time of casting lots, Abdullah was a young and handsome man. Many girls wanted to marry him. Despite this, his father wanted him to get married to girl who was equally good for him. He came to Wahb, the leader of the Sons of the Zuhra tribe, and told them that they were interested in his daughter Amina. Regarding beauty, conduct, and descent, Amina was the best among the Quraysh girls. When Abdul Muttalib asked Wahb's daughter for her hand in marriage for his son Abdullah, Wahb said, "O son of my uncle, we received this offer before you. Amina's mother had a dream. According to her, a light entered our house, and its brightness reached the earth and the heavens. Also, I had a dream regarding our grandfather, Prophet Abraham, last night. He told me, 'I married Abdul Muttalib's son Abdullah and your daughter Amina. You should agree to it.' Since this morning, I have been under the influence of that dream. I was wondering when you would come over and propose."

Upon hearing those blessed words, Abdul Muttalib's joy was hard to describe, as he chanted, "Allahu Akbar, Allahu Akbar." A short while later, Abdul Muttalib's son Abdullah and Wahb's daughter Amina got married, so a new family was formed.

A while after the wedding ceremony, the light on Abdullah's forehead transferred to Amina. This meant that the blessed mother was pregnant with the Prophet Muhammad, peace and blessings be upon him. Abdullah, who was doing trade business, had gone to Damascus with a group recently. On his way home, he could not continue his journey because he got sick in Medina. Thereupon, the people in the caravan left Abdullah at his uncle's home in Medina.

The caravan arrived in Mecca, and the news about Abdullah's sickness reached Abdul Muttalib. When he received the news, Abdul Muttalib immediately sent his oldest son, Harith, to Medina. However, the second news from Medina was even more bitter. Due to his increased sickness, Abdullah died and the Prophet Muhammad, peace and blessings be upon him, lost his father before he even left his mother's womb. His father left this world without seeing Muhammad, not being able to even seat him on his lap once.

The bitter news not only saddened Abdul Muttalib and Amina, but all of Mecca, too. Since Abdullah was deeply loved by everybody, he was God-fearing, honest, and truthful. In addition to that, he was so young, but that was Allah's destiny for his life. The grieving Amina's tears did not cease for days. She was mourning after her husband's death that she lost at such a young age. She would not eat or drink. The best way to describe her is as though she were melting like a candle.

Only her son who was going to be born two months later stopped her tears. The glad tidings had already been whispered into her ears. In her dream, she saw that just before her delivery the blessed mother was told, "Surely, you are pregnant with the Master of the *Ummah*. When you give birth to him, name him Muhammad," and Amina was immediately affected by this incident. Now her dreams were ornamented with the Divine trust that she was carrying in her womb.

Allah's House

Not much time had passed since Abdullah's death, now Abdul Muttalib, who was in grief over his beloved son, was facing another distress. Abraha, the governor of Yemen at that time, gathered his army to destroy the Ka'ba in Mecca, which was the house of Allah. The fact that the Arabs visited the Ka'ba in such large groups made Abraha feel very indisposed, so he built a big church in his own land as an alternative to the Ka'ba. He mobilized all his troops and workers, and set to work immediately on an imposing and magnificent church. His intention was to turn the attention of the people who went to the Ka'ba to that church. For the most part though, no one paid attention to Abraha's church. People, as usual were hurrying to the Ka'ba for pilgrimage.

In the meantime, the Arabs began making fun of that church in their poetry readings. A man who heard that Abraha built the church to change the pilgrims' direction went secretly to that church and dirtied it. This incident was the last straw for Abraha. He immediately ordered the preparation of a large army.

He began threatening that he would pull the stones of the Ka'ba out one by one and destroy them all.

Then, he prepared an army of sixty thousand men and started marching towards Mecca. There was also a huge elephant called Mahmud in the army. When the army approached Mecca, Abraha's soldiers began to raid Quraysh's goods. They even confiscated two hundred camels of Abdul Muttalib, who was the head of Mecca at the time. Upon hearing about the power of the approaching army, the people of Mecca understood that they did not have much of a chance, and started to wait with hopelessness. After a while, Abraha sent his delegate to Abdul Muttalib with the following message: "I did not come to fight you. The only reason I came is to destroy the Ka'ba. If you do not oppose me, I will have nothing to do with you and I will not harm you."

Upon receiving this message, Abdul Muttalib said, "I swear to Allah that it is not our intention to fight him. We do not have the strength for that anyway. However, this house is Allah's house. If he wishes, then he will definitely protect it. If he wills it to be destroyed, then we have no chance to protect it today." Afterwards, he went to Abraha with his delegate.

When Abraha saw Abdul Muttalib, he was impressed with his imposing stance. He entertained Abdul Muttalib royally. He came down from his high seat and sat down together with Abdul Muttalib on the floor. He asked with the help of his translator, "What do you want from me?"

"I want you to return my two hundred camels that your soldiers plundered," replied Abdul Muttalib.

Abraha was confused. What kind of a leader was he? He was threatening to destroy his land, but he was after his own property. He did not care about what was going to happen. He could not hide his feelings and said, "To tell you the truth, I was very impressed with you at first. However, the more I talk to you, the more I understand that you are not the man

Prophet Muhammad: The Seal of All Prophets

I thought you were. I am telling you that I came to destroy your Ka'ba, and all you care about are your camels."

With great seriousness, Abdul Muttalib said the following phrase, word for word: "I am just the owner of the camels. The owner of the Ka'ba is Allah. Surely, He will protect his house!"

Abraha was very angry. He shouted with anger, "Nobody is able to protect it against me! Nobody!"

Without changing his attitude, Abdul Muttalib in return said, "If so, then there is Him and there is you."

The atmosphere tensed up almost immediately. Abraha, who had become furious at the response he received, gave Abdul Muttalib his camels and sent him away. After returning to Mecca, Abdul Muttalib gathered his people and warned them of Abraha's threat and advised them to escape to the mountains to save their lives. On the other side, Abraha prepared his army and ordered them to destroy the Ka'ba. However, some men in his army would not obey his orders. A man named Nufayl, who was appointed to command the elephants, whispered into the biggest elephant ear, Mahmud, who was expected to do a great job, "Kneel down where you are and do not stand back up! Then go back to the place that you were born –Because you are in a blessed land."

He then departed and took refuge in the mountains. Indeed, as a miracle from Allah, Mahmud knelt down, and despite all the stress put on him, he refused to stand. No matter what, he would not walk towards Mecca. However, when his direction was changed, he would jump and start running. It was the same condition when his direction was changed to the left and right. The only direction the elephant would not go was towards the Ka'ba. To make him do what they wanted, they beat and harassed the poor animal, but the result did not change. Mahmud's whole body was drenched in blood, but he still did not march on to the Ka'ba.

While Abraha and his troops were still baffled in shock from the present situation, as time passed, they saw a dark silhouette was coming toward them from the coast side. When it got closer, they realized it was a large flock of birds. Each of these birds was known as *Ababil*, and was carrying three stones, holding one with its beak and the other two with its feet. Every stone they threw hit a soldier spot on, and the soldier hit by a stone fell to the ground instantly. The army was terrified and scared to death. While they were running around screaming, each of them died from being hit by stones.

Abraha had his share as well. While escaping, his body began to flake from the effect of a stone that hit him. He breathed his last breath in big agony and fear. The army that deliberately tried to destroy Allah's house had been shattered and torn apart. Soon, it started raining cats and dogs. The flood carried away the bodies of the disbeliever's army to the sea. Thus, just before the birth of the Messenger of Messengers, no damage was caused to the sacred house of Allah, the Ka'ba. The Ka'ba that was built by Prophet Abraham and his son Ishmael years ago who had plead to Allah, "Bring forth a Muslim nation from our descent," was now waiting for the Last Prophet.

The Ka'ba, which had been frequented by the Prophets since Adam, became a center of gloom. In this holy town, where one should be closest to Allah, everything that took people away from Allah was found. People left the religion of the Prophet Abraham, forgot the Lord of the Heavens, and made gods of wood and stone for themselves. They prostrated with such great respect in front of these inanimate idols that did not even bring themselves benefit, and were offering sacrifices to them. They even took it as far as filling every part of the Ka'ba with these idols.

The world had been facing a huge collapse in terms of religion, and Hijaz got its share too. People were assessed according to their material possessions, whereas the homeless were absolutely ignored. Rights and law were brutally forced out. The society was divided into classes. The condition of slaves was miserable. It had taken its toll on the institution of marriage. A woman was a worthless object. The fate of most of the girls was to be buried in the hot sands at very young ages so that they would be killed.

However, despite all that, there were people in Mecca who did not smudge the dirt of ignorance, who lived in this city that was home to ignorant and cruel beings. But these people were few in number. Some of the few were Quss ibn Saida, Waraqa ibn Nawfal, and Zayd ibn Amr. They were disturbed by what was happening around them, but they could not think of any solutions. The only hope these people who knew the holy books very well was the last Prophet. They accessed sources like the Torah and the Bible and came across signs of the last Prophet, who was going to enlighten the darkness. The glad tiding of the last Prophet that was going to be from the Prophet Abraham's descendant was circulating. It was as if the world was thirsty for the noble Prophet.

The Blessed Birth

About fifty days passed since Abraha attacked the Ka'ba. It was Monday, April 20th, 571. Dawn was about to break and the soon to be beloved Muhammad was about to enter the world. When his mother Amina was about to give birth, she heard an extremely loud and terrifying sound. When white birds came and stroked her back, her fear and grief vanished. As soon as she drank the sherbet that was served in a white bowl, her body was filled with heavenly light. Muhammad, the Pride of Humanity, peace and blessings be upon him, then came into this world.

When the beloved mother Amina heard and saw that she had given birth, she sat up straight to see her beloved newborn only to see him prostrating. This had to be an implication of some sort. The midwife, Shifa, who was present at the birth, heard him saying, "My Ummah, my Ummah!" Also, his index finger was lifted. Suddenly, the room was lit up and the whole world was filled with light. The stars in the sky had been lying in bunches and seemed as if they were raining on them. The mark between his shoulder blades had caught everyone's attention. The mark woven with black and yellow hair was the seal of Prophethood of the last Prophet expected in the near future.

Immediately after the blessed birth, the glad tidings were delivered to the Prophet's grandfather. Abdul Muttalib, who was at the Ka'ba when it happened, came home running. He took his grandson in his arms. He kissed him and loved him. He could not stop his tears. When it came to naming the baby, the respected Amina told Abdul Muttalib about the dream she had when she was pregnant and they named the rose-scented baby "Muhammad." Then Abdul Muttalib, with the orphan of his most beloved son Abdullah, went to the Ka'ba to thank to his Lord. His blessed grandson was sitting on his lap. The Ka'ba, the house of Allah, had met for the first time with Allah's most beloved servant.

The wonders that took place during the birth of the Master of mankind were not limited to the inside of the house. First, Mecca was shaken by the news that the idols in the Ka'ba fell head first to the ground that night. Nobody knew by whom and how this could have even happened. Then, one after the other, the news began to spread in various different places. The experiences were practically saying in their own languages, "Welcome!" to the last Sultan. The night of the blessed birth, a new star had shone and a Jewish scholar saw it dealing with the knowledge of stars in Mecca. In the morning, cutting off the path of Quraysh, he asked, "Has a male child been born in your tribe last night?"

Nobody had any idea yet that Abdul Muttalib's daughter in law, Amina, had given birth.

"We don't know of any," they answered.

The Jewish scholar said, "Then go and find out. Last night and this morning, the star of the last Prophet shone. There will be the seal of Prophethood on his back."

The Quraysh investigated the news and came back to the Jew and said, "Yes, Abdullah from our tribe had a son last night. In addition to this, he has the seal on his back."

The Jew, who could not believe his ears, wished to go and see the blessed baby. Coming into his presence, he felt as though he was going crazy when he also saw the seal of Prophethood on his back. While quickly running away, he was shouting, "The Quraysh will receive such a state in the future that the news will spread everywhere, from east to west. Prophethood is now gone from the children of Israel, it's gone!"

The news that came from Iran, one of the greatest states in its time was interesting. Four towers of the palace of the Persian Ruler (Kisra), which were pretty strong, cracked and collapsed the minute the Master was born. Both the Persian Ruler and the people waited for morning to understand what was happening. When dawn came, they saw in horror that fourteen of the strong towers collapsed. The Persian Ruler called the clergy and asked what was happening. Just when the clergy arrived, a Messenger could be seen in the distance. That same night, flame of the fire worshipping Iranians, which had not extinguished for centuries, was also extinguished. While his eyes grew wider with excitement, the Persian Ruler asked his head judge, "What does it all mean?"

The head judge had also seen an interesting dream recently. With a thoughtful tone in his voice, he said, "It seems that important tasks will be accomplished by Arabs."

They then sought after somebody and found one to resolve the situation. After listening to what was happening, a scholar named Satih, who lives in Damascus said, "Revelation will start descending from the heaven and the Last Prophet will arrive, and the Persian Ruler will lose his kingship."

Indeed, sixty-seven years later, the news that was being reported was exactly what the scholar had described.

In the Land of the Wet Nurse

For a healthier environment, hiring a wet nurse for their newborns out of town had become a custom of the Meccans. Since Mecca had a hot and muggy climate. Moreover, some tribes outside Mecca lived a decent life without being affected by the ugliness of the age of ignorance. Through different times in the years, wet nurses from these tribes would come to Mecca and take newborn babies and go back to their homes. In return for money, gifts, and some merchandise, they wet-nursed the babies for two-three years.

There was a plateau near Mecca where Arabic was spoken in a very beautiful way and the children were taught high morality. But that year, an unprecedented drought occurred in the plateau where the Sons of Sa'd had been living. The long-standing Amina burned up all bits and pieces. The milk of the wet nurses who did not have enough food was quite low. However, the women of this tribe came to Mecca that year too, despite the hard conditions. They were going to take few nurslings in order to help contribute to their income. Harith, from the land of the Sons of Sa'd, his wife Halima, and ten women all went on their way to Mecca for that very reason. However, Halima's bony donkey and Harith's old camel had difficulty walking, and the family of Harith could not keep up with their friends. When they arrived in Mecca, their travelling Companions had already picked the children they wanted to nurture.

Halima and Harith started wandering in search of nurslings. The only child that had not been given to a wet nurse was the orphan child Muhammad of Abdullah. Whoever found out he was an orphan child, did not want to take him and turned to another child. Halima, who saw that children of wealthy families were already shared among other women, was upset. She did not want to go back home without bringing a child with her, especially since she had come such a long distance. While walking absent minded on the streets of Mecca, a tall and imposing man came along. It was Abdul Muttalib, the leader of the Quraysh tribe. He asked Halima, "Which tribe are you from?"

"From the Bakr tribe."

"What's your name?" was his next question.

"Halima."

"Where you come from, the children are well taken care of. They are being taught high morality. O Halima, I have an offer for you!"

Halima looked curiously at Abdul Muttalib and started waiting for the offer without saying a single word. Our Prophet Muhammad's grandfather sighed and continued, "I have an orphan grandchild. I offered him to other women before you, but they did not take him. Please, come and take him as your nursling. Thus, maybe Allah will bring grace and abundance to your home."

This offer immediately went into Halima's mind, as she did not want to go back home without a single child. Instead of accepting the offer right away, Halima walked away saying that she had to ask her husband's opinion. After explaining to Harith what had happened, she said, "My intention is to go and get that child. I don't want to go back without taking a nursling. Now tell me your opinion too!"

"Let's do it! Perhaps Allah will bestow His blessings on us for his sake," said Harith.

When the couple came back and told Abdul Muttalib that they accepted his offer, the Quraysh leader was pleased. He prayed for them and immediately took Halima to our mother, Amina's house. At that moment, our Master, the Sultan of the Universe was sleeping in his crib. There was a very nice smell around him. Halima, who took the baby in her arms with permission from Amina, started nursing the baby immediately. Her breasts, which did not have any milk at that moment, were welled up with milk. The Master of Masters then Halima's son Abdullah both sucked milk from her breast until they were full. Both of them fell asleep. However, Abdullah could not fall asleep for days due to his hunger.

They spent that night in Mecca. The next day they were going to take their nurslings and return home. When they came up to their old camel they saw that his breasts were also welled up with milk. They milked the camel and drank it until they were full. The night that they spent in Mecca was their happiest and most blessed night all throughout their lives. And this blessing never fell short so long as the Master of Masters remained in their presence.

The beloved Amina was very sad leaving her rose-scented baby. She hugged her only son in tears and looked at him tenderly for a long time. She prayed to her Lord silently that nothing bad should happen to the blessed baby given into the custody of Harith and Halima.

When Halima took the Master of Masters in her lap and mounted on the donkey, all of a sudden the weak and bony donkey changed. The donkey started walking very fast. The donkey had been moving so fast that they had practically caught up with their friends, who had set off days before them. Even though their travelling Companions were tired and exhausted, Halima and Harith were quite vigorous. Their friends didn't understand this at all. Soon, they turned to Halima, and said, "What does this mean Halima? Weren't you always behind us and were late?" They could not help asking her if this was the donkey that she had been riding days before.

Halima and Harith were aware that the blessings that were being granted to them were due to the nursling that they had brought home with them from Mecca. There was a different type of abundance in their soils, which were considered to be droughty and unproductive. Their sheep started to produce more milk. The other herd owners were even calling their shepherds and scolding them by saying, "Shame on you! Why don't you bring your herds to where Halima's sheep are grazing? We wish our sheep looked as nice and had as much milk as Halima's sheep."

Similar conversations took place regularly between herd owners and shepherds. Because of their weakness, animals in the upland looked like they were starving. Drought and famine got so bad, that they decided to perform the Prayer for rain. It was Friday. Everybody, families and singles, all moved up to the high hill. Accompanied by an old priest, they prayed for hours. However, there wasn't even a small raindrop falling down from the sky. People in the upland grew very sad, but they kept waiting helplessly. At that moment, an old lady dodged through the crowd and approached the priest. She said, "There is a Meccan boy in our neighbor Halima's house. They have received many blessings after he entered their house. I say that we should bring this child here and pray for the sake of his Lord. Then the Lord of the Worlds will most probably bestow rain on us."

The priest found this idea very logical. In fact, they did not have any hopes other than that. The old lady found Halima in the crowd and told her the situation. Because it was very hot that day, Halima did not bring the blessed baby to the hill. They returned home together with the old lady. Halima wrapped her beloved nursling in a blanket and put a piece of cloth on his face to protect him from the sunlight. They immediately left her house. They wanted to reach the hill without wasting any time. While approaching the gathering place, they realized that a small cloud was shading them. The cloud followed them through their walk. The priest also realized it as he had been watching them after they had left home. He also started to think that this Meccan child would bring them blessings. He took the Messenger of Allah from Halima's lap and shouted to the crowd, "O people! Ask for rain from your Lord for this child's sake. This child is a beloved one in the sight of Allah."

Somehow, he could not take his eyes off the Prophet's black eyes. During Prayers, the small cloud shading Allah's Messenger covered the whole sky and grew very dark. It was the awaited time. Suddenly, everybody started cheering joyfully, "Rain, it's raining! It's raining!"

It rained discontinuously for exactly one week. Pastures turned green, water supplies were full, and trees started shooting. Animals were full and produced more milk. The blessings in Halima's house spread across the upland.

Meanwhile, two years had passed. Allah's Messenger grew up and became a robust child. At this time, he was not being nursed. The time period, upon which Halima, Amina, and Abdul Muttalib agreed, was over, and it was time to say farewell. As they promised, they took little Muhammad to his mother in Mecca. Coming together with her dear son, Amina began crying out of happiness. She smelled him over again while hugging him firmly. But Halima was very sad. She did not want to leave her beloved nursling. Her heart was full of sorrow. She felt like something inside her was broken, when she remembered that she was going to leave him. She asked Amina like she was begging, "I am worried that he will catch the Meccan plague here. I wish that he stays with us just a little longer."

Amina opposed the idea of leaving her son right after coming back together. However, she was also worried that he would catch the epidemic disease in Mecca. She accepted the offer reluctantly. Halima and Harith took their nursling back again and returned home joyfully.

Allah's Messenger spent most of his time with his foster sisters and brothers. Both, his foster mother and father loved him a lot and coddled him. They spent two more years together that way. One day, Allah's Messenger was playing with his foster sisters and brothers in the back of their house. Suddenly, Halima's son Abdullah came running to his mother. He excitedly said, "Two men clothed in white put my foster brother Muhammad on the ground and split his belly."

Halima and Harith were very scared. Running, they went to where Abdullah told them. Their foster son's face was really pale. He was just standing. First Halima and then Harith

Prophet Muhammad: The Seal of All Prophets

hugged Muhammad. They asked him, "What happened to you?"

The Prophet started to tell them what had happened: "Two men in white attire came to me. One of them had a golden bowl filled with snow. They made me gently lay down on the ground. They opened my chest, took my heart out, and split it into two pieces. They removed a black clot from it. Then they washed my heart and belly with icy snow until they had thoroughly cleaned it. After that, one of them said to the other one 'Put him on a scale and ten people of his Ummah (community) against him.' They weighed me against ten people and I outweighed them. Afterwards, he repeated, 'Weigh him against a hundred people.' They weighed me against hundred people and I outweighed them again. He said this time, 'Weigh him against a thousand people of his community.' I was weighed against a thousand people and I outweighed them. When he saw this, he said, 'Leave him! I swear by Allah, if you weighed him against all of his people, he would outweigh them.'"

Halima and Harith were very anxious. When they returned home, Harith said, "O Halima! I fear that something bad may happen to him. If you agree, we should probably take him back to his family in Mecca."

Halima agreed to this idea. It was best to give the entrusted child back to his mother as soon as possible. Thus, they immediately set off for Mecca to bring their foster son Muhammad to his mother, Amina. The Prophet's days in his foster mother's home came to an end, when he was around four years old.

Farewell to Mom

After this incident, Allah's Messenger lived with his mother. He was the dearest one in the family. Amina was trying to make her son not feel his father's absence. His grandfather and uncles also had a share in this, as they all looked after him too.

When the Prophet was six years old, Amina decided to go to Medina to visit her relatives and her late husband, Abdullah's grave, so that she would pray for him there for. She set off with her servant, Umm Ayman, and her beloved son. When they reached Medina, Allah's Messenger was destitute. He visited his father's grave—he never saw him alive —and for the first time ever, he felt it in his heart that he was an orphan. Tears falling from his blessed eyes wet the soil on his father's grave.

After a short time, Amina got sick during this visit and day-by-day, her disease became more serious. They immediately set out to return to Mecca. When they arrived near a village called Abwa, Amina didn't have any energy to even take one step. They took a break under a tree. Apparently, the blessed mother was about to say goodbye. Her eyes were on her rosy-faced son. She was burning inside because she had to leave her already fatherless son motherless as well. She constantly wept. Seeing her like this made Umm Ayman and Allah's Messenger cry, too. His head was on his mother's knees. Allah's Messenger could not stop his tears.

He was frequently asking, "Mommy, how do you feel?"

Amina felt a deep pang of sadness, when she saw her son in tears. Gasping for a final breath, she said to her son, "If what I had dreamt is true, you are the last Messenger who will be sent to all creatures and all humanity. You will complete what Prophet Abraham brought and you will venture away from worshiping idols. Every living being must eventually die. Everything new must eventually get old. I am dying today. But my name shall remain. Because I gave birth to a pure child and I have left behind abundant goodness."

After saying these last words, she looked at her son's bright face for the last time, and then she passed away. She had taken her last breath. From then on, he was an orphan, both fatherless and motherless. He was feeling a sense of sorrow, which could not be described with words. They buried Amina with the help of other people. Allah's Messenger and Umm Ayman then returned to Mecca.

The Trust of Abdullah

After bringing the Prophet to his grandfather, Umm Ayman told him in detail what had happened during the journey. Abdul Muttalib became very sad upon learning about his daughter-in-law's death. His grandchild had never seen his father and now his mother passed away, too. He looked at his light-faced grandson sadly. He would take the trust of Abdullah under his protection. He was trying to make him not feel the absence of his parents. He was spoiling him so much. When he went somewhere, he took his grandson with him. He let him in to the meetings with leaders in Mecca and sometimes he was even asking his ideas about the issues.

One day, Abdul Muttalib went to Yemen with his delegation in Quraysh. During this visit the Abyssinian ruler Sayf took a close interest in Abdul Muttalib. But his interest did not go unnoticed. When they were alone together, he used the opportunity to talk to Abdul Muttalib privately. He said, "O Abdul Muttalib! I shall tell you some secrets. I think that this concerns you, so I will tell it to you only. Don't mention what I tell you to anyone until Allah wills. We learned from our holy books that a child will be born and he will have a mole between his shoulders as a sign for his prophecy. He will claim your leadership until the Judgment Day. Now it is time that he comes up to the world. His name will be Muhammad.

Both parents will die at a young age. First, his grandfather and then his uncle will be his guardians. We have been talking to each other about his coming up. He will break the idols, and the fire-temples will be extinguished with his prophecy. O Abdul Muttalib! You are this child's grandfather."

Abdul Muttalib was not surprised by what he was told. He nodded slowly and then said, "O King! It is true that I had a son. I loved him a lot and coddled him. I made him marry with Wahb's daughter, Amina, who was the noblest among other girls in our tribe. Soon, after he passed away. Amina was pregnant. After a short time, Amina gave birth to a baby boy and I named him Muhammad. Yet, his mother died not long ago. I have taken the responsibility of raising him."

Sayf impatiently said, "This is what I was trying to tell you. O Abdul Muttalib! Protect him well. If I had known that I would live until then, I would have settled in Medina with my army and waited for him. Because I see in the holy books that he will settle in Medina and his helpers and grave will both be there."

The delegation of Quraysh got their job done and returned to Mecca. Abdul Muttalib's preoccupation was with what Sayf had told him. It was obvious that his noble grandson would have a different future. The compassionate grandfather couldn't help imagine what those days would hold. Indeed, the good news he heard about his grandson was not limited to what Sayf told him. The ones who read the holy books and went into more depth in religion knew that Abdullah's trust, Muhammad, was the awaited last Prophet and all of them told that it was necessary to protect him from the evil of jealous religious scholars. Abdul Muttalib thought that he should be more careful about his rosy-faced grandson. He wasn't his son's trust only, but he was also the Prophet for whom everybody had been waiting.

Allah's Messenger reached the age of eight. After Abdullah and Amina's death, Abdul Muttalib was also preparing to say his farewells to the world. He felt as though they were his last days. He had his mind on his orphan son. One day, he called Abu Talib, one of his sons, and said to him, "This son's laurels will be exalted. He is a trust from me to you." Saying this, he entrusted his beloved grandson to his most compassionate son, Abu Talib.

Soon after, he passed away when he was about eighty-two years old. When the Prophet heard that his grandfather breathed his last breathe, he shed tears for a long time right beside his grandfather's dead body. His grandfather, who protected him all the time with his compassion, loved him most and so made him feel this love without stint, was not living anymore.

The Uncle's Protection

Seeing Allah's Messenger like this, by the side of his grandfather, affected his uncle Abu Talib deeply. He was his brother's trust and his father's last will. He hugged the Prophet as tenderheartedly as a father. Soon after, Allah's Messenger felt as though his uncle, Abu Talib, was his father, and that his wife, Fatima, was his mother.

Abu Talib was a poor man, but after his nephew Muhammad came to their house, there was a special abundance and grace found at home. When the family members sat down to a meal in the absence of Allah's Messenger, they had to finish their meal without being full. However, when they ate together with him, they witnessed that the meal had increased and remained. Abu Talib loved his nephew more than his own kids. He showed interest and affection in him more than anyone else. He kept him insight and he preferred to go everywhere with him.

Abu Talib was a tradesman, like many Qurayshi people. Those days, he decided to participate in the caravan travelling from Mecca to Damascus. He expected to earn some money with this business, so that he could better their living conditions. He was often thinking about taking Allah's Messenger with him. Because he was worried that something could happen to him. He did not want to take him out of Mecca. But when he was ready to leave, Allah's Messenger came to his uncle and said, "O Uncle! To whom are you leaving me here? I have neither a mother nor a father."

After saying these, he started to cry. Abu Talib got very sad and said, "Well then, my beloved Muhammad. You come with me too. Don't cry anymore."

After they prepared everything for the trip, they set off. When the trade caravan traveled some distance, they stopped over in Busra. There was a Christian priest called Bahira living in the monastery of Busra. That day, while the caravan was approaching Busra, he saw that a cloud was following the caravan, and it was shading someone in particular. "There should be somebody extraordinary in this caravan. I wonder whether this person is the last Prophet heralded in the holy books." He had such thoughts in his mind. Bahira grew extremely excited and desired to find out this miracle's secret that he invited the people in the caravan for a meal when they came in front of the monastery. Everybody, except Allah's Messenger, participated in the meal. Bahira looked at everyone carefully. When he couldn't see the features mentioned in the holy books on any of them, he immediately asked, "Is there anyone in the caravan left behind?"

One of them said, "There is no one left behind except a child."

Bahira said, "Please bring him here! He should eat, too."

One of them went to Allah's Messenger and called him. They then found their way back to the monastery together.

When the Priest Bahira saw Allah's Messenger, he immediately realized that he was the heralded last Prophet. He said to the Prophet, "O Child! I am going to ask you some questions. Answer me for the sake of the gods Lat and Uzza!"

"Don't ask me anything for the sake of Lat and Uzza! I don't hate anything more than them," abruptly replied the Messenger.

"So, answer my questions for Allah's sake!"

"You can ask me anything you wish!" he said.

Thereupon, Bahira asked the Messenger of Allah many questions. The Prophet answered all the questions honestly and without asking anything in return. All his features matched the Prophet's description written in the holy books. After asking a few questions, Bahira checked his back and saw the seal of the prophecy between his shoulders. He was now sure that he was the awaited last Prophet. Turning to Abu Talib, he asked, "What is this child's relationship to you?"

"He is my son," replied Abu Talib.

Bahira confidently said, "He is not your son! His father cannot be living."

When he said this, Abu Talib answered, "You're right. He is my brother's son."

Bahira continued his questions, "What happened to his father?"

"He died when his mother was pregnant with him."

"You have told the truth," replied Bahira. "What happened to his mother?"

"She died when Muhammad was six years old."

After Abu Talib's responses, the Priest Bahira drew himself closer to him and said, "You have said the truth! Take Muhammad back to your hometown, because this child is the last Prophet among all other Prophets. Jews have hoped that the last Prophet will rise from amongst their nation. If they realize that this child is the last Prophet, they might kill him because of their jealousy. He is not of Jewish descent."

Full of love for his nephew, Abu Talib followed Bahira's advice and the caravan did not go any further. They sold their goods there in Busra. Then they immediately returned to Mecca.

Far from Sins

After their talk with Bahira, Abu Talib was much more cautious about his nephew. Meanwhile, Allah's Messenger grew older and taller. He attracted attention with his figure. His behaviors and manners were very different than others' general customs. He had a very pure life under the protection of his Lord all the time. When there was a good deed to perform, he was always the first to help. He was far from all kinds of evils. In addition to not having a tendency to any bad habits, he hated idols. However, the Meccan people had a close relationship with idols in their daily lives. Darkness and ignorance were ruling over Mecca. People were wasting their lives by associating partners with the Lord of the Worlds. They worshipped idols made of stones and woods. Two of them were regarded as their greatest gods: Lat and Uzza. Meccans swore by them and asked others to swear by them, too.

One of these lifeless idols was standing in a place called Buwana in Mecca. Meccan people considered this idol as one of the greatest, and visited it on certain days in the year. They sacrificed here and they made wishes encircling around this idol. It was a festival day. Abu Talib asked Muhammad to go to Buwana with him, as he always wanted to keep his nephew nearby. Allah's Messenger refused this meaningless request without hesitation, but Abu Talib did not like this. At that moment the Prophet's aunts intervened and said to him,

"O Muhammad! Why do you refuse to come with us on the day of festival? What do you want to do? Surely, we are afraid that something might happen to you, because you are keeping yourself so far away from them."

Our beloved Prophet felt suffocated in these conversations and he immediately left. He did not want to go to a place where lifeless idols were associated partners with the Creator of everything, so he desired to stay alone. He returned home in a hurry after a very short time. Seeing him in such a state, his aunts anxiously asked him, "O Muhammad! What made you so scared?"

"I fear that something may happen to me."

"Allah will not test you with evil. We witness that you are full of good."

Then he said, "Every time when I got closer to your idols, a tall and white-dressed man appeared in front of me and cried, "O Muhammad! Don't approach them and stay where you are."

It was the last conversation between Allah's Messenger and his relatives about idols. Seeing his different states, his relatives did not force him to approach the idols again. Being under Divine protection, the Prophet's youth was far away from evil and sins. Whenever he met something against Allah's commands, his Lord always protected him.

Allah's Messenger was different from his peers in all his behaviors and manners. He was now twenty years old and he gained the Meccan people's appreciation for his wonderful manners. His attitudes towards events, his interpretations, and his right decisions made him a source of appeal to others. He was known for his high morality and trustworthiness. As a result, the Meccan people started calling him Muhammad'ul-Amin (Muhammad, the Trustworthy). The people in his immediate circle were decent people like him. He preferred being with them or being alone. He never approached any kind of ignorant customs. His closest friend was Abu Quhafa's son Abu Bakr , may Allah be pleased with him. Abu Bakr was two years younger than Allah's Messenger. He had a great respect for the Prophet, and he took him to be his example and role model. Because they were very similar with respect to their character and their moral values, they grew very fond of each other and became very close friends. They grew up together, and the people of Mecca were used to seeing these two friends together.

Unlike them, a few people who had high moral values, ignorance was getting worse among others during those years in Mecca. There was no life safety in the city, particularly for foreigners and poor people. Foreign traders' merchandise especially was taken by force and they were not paid for. People were victimized openly in those days. One day, a merchant from Yemen brought goods on a camel into Mecca. One of the leaders in Mecca (his name was As) purchased these goods, but did not pay for them and he denied his liability. The foreigner became wretched and he did not know what to do. He consulted some arbiter families in Mecca. But he could not receive any support. Nobody wanted to object to As. The desperate merchant climbed to the Mountain of Abu Qubays against the Ka'ba and started to shriek.

Such unfairness was the straw that broke the camel's back. Zubayr, the Prophet's uncle, was the first one who took action first to help this poor merchant. He came nearby and said to him,

"What happened to you? Why are you so sad?"

The man was really afflicted. Meeting someone who cared about his situation, he started to tell his story from the beginning. Thereupon, representatives of dignitary families in Mecca gathered in a house. After having a meal together, they talked about the unjust events in Mecca. Finally, they decided to take precautions against the oppression of residents and foreigners and prevent any kind of injustice. Then they covenanted to get innocent's rights from tyrant and provide justice as a result. This event was a big step at the time. Because human rights were disregarded, powerful people were considered to be right all the time, and weak people were despised. Allah's Messenger was one of the participants of this meeting. This decision was put into effect with the merchant's trouble that cried at the Mountain of Abu Qubays. As was then forced to pay his dues to the downtrodden merchant after all the dignitaries in Mecca opposed him.

Meanwhile, an unexpected event took place in Mecca. A war exploded between the tribe of Kinanah, including the Quraysh, and the Banu Qays. This war occurred in the month of Muharram, a month that Arabs considered sacred, and bloodshed and war were considered sins. Due to that, this war was called the Fijar War, which means The Sacrilegious War. Allah's Messenger was also present in this war; however, he did not kill a single person. He just picked up the arrows that fell around him and gave them to his uncles. But many people were killed in this war. Those were some of the hardest times. Eventually, someone from Quraysh invited both sides to a ceasefire while everybody was tired of this meaningless war. This offer was accepted. After the war had ended, there was peace again in Mecca.

The Heralded Prophet

Almost four more years went by and Allah's Messenger had turned twenty-five years old. During that time, people were preparing a trade caravan for a journey to Damascus. The owner of this caravan was Khadija, may Allah be pleased with her, who was one of the wealthiest ladies in Mecca. She was looking for a trustworthy person for the caravan who could do business on her behalf. Therefore, she sent her servants to begin the search. She chose someone from the candidates and then sent him to Damascus.

The Prophet's uncle Abu Talib was also one of those who heard this news. He rushed toward his nephew and said to him, "O my brother's son! I am a person who does not have any property anymore. We have neither our wealth nor a business left. There is a caravan from your tribe right here ready to go to Damascus. Khadija is looking for someone who can carry out her business for her. Even though I do not want you to go to Damascus, lest someone there might bring you harm, we don't have any other choice. If you go to Khadija, she would surely choose you, because you are trustworthy and your nature is pure."

Allah's Messenger looked at his uncle as if to say, "Whatever you like." Abu Talib went to see Khadija when he got an affirmative answer from his nephew. He felt a need to tell her about his nephew personally. After all, he was Muhammad, the Trustworthy. He was the most trusted person in Mecca. Abu Talib thought that this should be taken into consideration when hiring him and his wage should be different from others. Abu Talib asked Khadija his nephew's wage. In no time, he was with Khadija. They inquired after each other and then they started to talk about the caravan going to Damascus. Abu Talib mentioned to Khadija that he was thinking of his nephew Muhammad to run her business. After that, he started to tell her his nephew's virtues at length.

The moment Khadija had been waiting for a long time was about to occur. In fact, her unique desire was to know Allah's Messenger better. Khadija became a widow at an early age. She was a matchless lady in Mecca in terms of her wealth, honor, and nobility. Even in those times of ignorance, when women were devalued and looked down upon, she organized caravans and conducted international trade. She was far from the ignorance in Mecca and she was one from the people of good morality. Her cousin, Waraqa ibn Nawfal, known for his piety, was her important helper and biggest source of information.

Waraqa had always thought that worshiping idols was wrong, and he was looking for the right religion. He could read and understand the Torah and the Bible in their original Hebrew language. He knew Judaism and Christianity very well. His searching led him to his knowledge about the last Prophet foretold in the scriptures. He was always mentioning a Prophet that was to arrive soon. In fact, the arrival of the last Prophet was not only a mention of Waraqa. It was actually a common matter in all of the Arabian Peninsula. Khadija was one of them who firmly believed that the last Prophet would arrive soon.

Once, she dreamt of a strong light, like the moon or the sun, came into her house and into her bosom, radiating out and enlightening the whole universe. The old Waraqa was astounded when he heard Khadijah's dream. In great excitement, he said, "Glad tidings to you, dear cousin! May good things come upon you, my uncle's daughter! This dream is undoubtedly a sign of Allah's bounty to you. Soon, Allah will grant your home Divine light. Of course, Allah knows best, but I think this may be the light of the prophecy or a Prophet only."

Khadija was so amazed by what she had heard from Waraqa. He continued talking, "The Last Prophet has entered the world. You will be among his family. In your lifetime, he will receive Divine revelation and his religion will encompass the entire universe. You will be the first of his believers. This Prophet will be among the Quraysh and from the family of Hashim."

Khadija had many other dreams that we similar to this one. In addition to her dreams and Waraqa's interpretations, some other unexpected and extraordinary events also occurred in those days. It took place on a festival day. The Meccan ladies were sitting together somewhere close to the Ka'ba, celebrating the festival amongst them. Khadija had completed her circumambulation of the Ka'ba and was praying to her Lord. She then joined a group of ladies sitting down nearby. Not long after, a man whom they did not recognize had appeared. When he approached them, he raised his voice by saying, "O Meccan women! O Meccan women!"

Then he continued, "There is no doubt that a Messenger will come up from your city. His name is Ahmad. Whoever has a chance to marry him should say 'yes' to him without hesitation."

Most of the women who heard him thought that the man was crazy. Therefore, they continued their work, telling him to 'cut the nonsense,' and some threw stones at him, calling him a "lunatic." It was obvious that he was referring to Khadija. Indeed, she was the only lady that took the man's words seriously.

All Khadija heard about the Last Prophet until that point propelled her having expectations and seeking him. She was constantly thinking of it and looking for someone matching the information she had already received. There were only a handful of moral people in those times when the ignorance kept worsening. Thus, Khadija did not have any difficulties in finding the right address. At that time in Mecca, there was only one person who fit all the described features. He was Abdullah's son, Muhammad'ul-Amin, known for his honesty and trustworthiness. After all, Khadija started to examine his life and personality.

With Abu Talib's offer, she met Allah's Messenger unexpectedly while looking for him. This business could be a great opportunity to get to know him better. She was very pleased with the offer. Even if Abu Talib had asked her to give all her wealth as a wage, she would have given it without hesitation. For this, Khadija answered Abu Talib with these words,

"O Abu Talib! Honestly, you asked for such a small and insignificant wage for him from me! If you had asked me more, I swear by Allah, I would have accepted your offer."

Finally, Abu Talib and Khadija came to an agreement. Muhammad'ul-Amin would be Khadija's representative for her caravan that was heading to Damascus. Khadija sent with him her most skilled and trusted servant, Maysara. Maysara would serve Allah's Messenger during their journey and report everything to Khadija when they returned. It was a great opportunity to get to know Muhammad'ul-Amin a little better. What this meant was that Maysara was actually entrusted with a very important task.

On the Way to Damascus

F inally, the journey that had lasted three months had commenced. During this journey, the people of the caravan got to know each other and had the opportunity to know what Allah's Messenger was like more closely. At the end of a tiring journey, they reached Busra, close to Damascus. Everyone was eager to sell what he or she had brought and to purchase new goods.

For a moment, Maysara caught a glimpse of a heated discussion between Muhammad'ul-Amin and another person. He had to understand what was happening, because when they returned, he would tell Khadija everything he observed. Getting closer, he realized that they were bargaining. The man was asking Muhammad'ul-Amin for an oath. But he was requesting him to swear upon the idols Lat and Uzza. With a steadfast tone of voice, Allah's Messenger said, "I will never swear by their names. Indeed, there is nothing that seems so unlovable to me as those idols."

The man, who saw the determination of Allah's Messenger, changed his mind about the pledge on the names of Lat and Uzza. They agreed on the Prophet's terms and finalized the business.

After Allah's Messenger left, the man came to Maysara and excitedly asked, "Who is this man not swearing by Lat and Uzza? Do you know him?"

Then he said without even awaiting Maysara's answer, "Do not leave his side. He is undoubtedly a Prophet."

At last, they finished their business in Damascus, and set off on their way back to Mecca. Everybody was resting. Allah's Messenger was also sitting and resting in the shade of an old olive tree. After a short time, a man came to them running and approached them gasping for air. This was none other than the famous Priest Nastura. He came to Maysara and asked,

"Who is that cooling off under that tree?"

Maysara said, "He is Muhammad, Abdullah's son. He is a youth from the family of Hashim."

Thereupon, Nastura said, "I swear that none other than a Prophet settled beneath that tree up until now!"

Then he asked for some characteristics about of Muhammad'ul-Amin. After hearing the answers he expected, he confidently said, "There is no doubt that he is the Prophet for whom this Ummah has been waiting. And he is the last of all Prophets."

The priest Nastura, however, could not leave. He wanted to get more information about him. That is why he kept asking Maysara about the Prophet resting under the tree, and wanted him to tell him everything that he had witnessed while accompanying the Messenger of Allah. Maysara told the priest of the event that had taken place in the market, when Allah's Messenger would not swear upon the idols. The priest was astonished and his excitement doubled. With absolute assurance, he said, "I swear that he is the awaited Prophet. Keep an eye on him!"

After having said this, he rushed towards Allah's Messenger and kissed him respectfully on his forehead, then bowed to his feet and said, "I bear witness that you are the last Prophet foretold in the Torah."

After a while, the caravan was ready to return to Mecca. Although the weather was very hot, two clouds appeared in the sky. Moreover, these clouds were following the caravan above the Prophet. When he stopped, they stopped, and when he continued moving, they followed him. Maysara was lost in astonishment. But the Messenger of Allah continued on his way resolutely, as if there were nothing out of the ordinary.

During the journey, there was not any wrongdoing or misgiving. They invested everything ideally, which they had taken to Damascus. What they brought to Mecca was sold at very good prices. It was obvious that Khadija would be very pleased because of this business. However, Khadija's concern was not how much profit she would have. She was waiting excitedly for the news Maysara would bring.

The caravan arrived in Mecca during the hottest hours of the day. That time, Khadija was sitting with some ladies and talking with them on the second floor of her house. One of the ladies saw the caravan entering the city and pointed it out. All the ladies looked outside. All attention was focused on Allah's Messenger. The ladies were watching him in wonder. Everyone was amazed to see that while Prophet was riding ahead on his camel, two clouds were following him and shielding him from sun.

Allah's Messenger arrived at Khadija's house. He reported how much they profited from the sales. After delivering to Khadija the merchandise they bought in Busra, he left. Then she immediately found Maysara, so that she could find out all of what he had witnessed on this journey. Maysara told her everything that had happened in detail. He could not say enough about him.

Indeed, it was what Khadija was expecting to hear. She was now sure that all the signs about the last Prophet was indicating that he was Muhammad, the Trustworthy. She rose and went directly to Waraqa. She told her cousin at once all the information that she had heard from Maysara. Waraqa was also excited by the news. Looking at Khadija carefully, he said,

"If all of what you said is true, o Khadija, there is no doubt that Muhammad is these people's Prophet. I also knew that this Ummah had an awaited Prophet. And this time is the time of his arrival."

Khadija no longer had any doubt. The heralded Prophet, for whom she had been waiting for years, was now very close to her. She could not think of any way to be closer to him besides marriage.

The Most Fortunate Lady Ever

Khadija had married twice before. She had closed the door to all proposals since then. She had received lots of proposals, but she refused all of them. The only solution was to be with the Messenger of Allah was getting married to him. Khadija, who had been planning not to get married again, had made up her mind. She had to marry Muhammad'ul-Amin, but she did not know how and whom to explain this. Pensively, she spent days thinking about this dilemma. Her close friend, Nafisa took notice of her thoughtful state. One day, she came nearby and asked her, "What happened to you, o Khadija? What is your problem? I have never seen you this preoccupied."

After remaining silent for a while, Khadija decided to tell her trouble to her best friend. Then she started telling, "There is no doubt that I see some superiority in Abdullah's son, Muhammad, which I have not seen in anyone before. He is honest, trustworthy, and an honorable person, and he comes from a noble and pure lineage. He is the best person that one could hope to meet. Moreover, there is good news about his future. My heart nearly stopped when I heard what Maysara witnessed in the market place, when I listened to what the priest told, and when I saw the cloud that followed him

on his return from Damascus. I believe that he is the awaited Prophet!"

Nafisa did not really understand what her friend was im-
plying.

"But what does all this have to do with the fact that you
are in deep thought?" asked Nafisa.

Khadija started to tell more openly,

"I hope that we can join our paths through marriage, but
I do not know how to go about it." This time, Nafisa compre-
hended her situation. She said, "If you allow me, I will talk to
him for you." Khadija answered with excitement, "If you can,
o Nafisa, hop to it and do it right away!"

In no time, Nafisa left Khadija's house. Before long, she
was with Allah's Messenger. First, she greeted him and afterwards, "O Muhammad! What withholds you from getting
married? Why don't you get married?" she asked.

This was a surprising question that Allah's Messenger
was not expecting.

"I do not have the means to get married," he said.

Nafisa said, "If financial means were not a matter and
there was someone equal to you in beauty, wealth, and hon-
or, would you like to get married to her?"

"So who is this person then?"

"Khadija."

"How could this happen?"

"You leave it to me. I will take care of it."

After Nafisa's last words, Allah's Messenger kept silent.
According to Nafisa, this silence was a sign that he was feeling and thinking thoughts about the proposal. Thereupon,

Nafisa left there quickly and she directly rushed to her friend Khadija. In one breath, Nafisa told her the conversation that she had with Allah's Messenger. This news Nafisa brought relieved Khadija. She immediately sent him a message concerning the matter, why she wanted to marry him. She started as follows, "O my uncle's son! There is no doubt that I am asking you for marriage because of our shared lineage, your incomparable status in your tribe, your good morals, and your trustworthiness. Tell your uncles to begin preparing."

Allah's Messenger did not want to decide without consulting his elders since the matter was very important. After receiving the proposal, he went to his uncle Abu Talib right away. He told his uncle about the conversation he had with Nafisa and mentioned Khadija's proposal. Abu Talib gave him permission to marry the Khadija, who was known at the time as "Tahira," meaning, "pure and clean lady," even in those days of ignorance. He thought that they were equal in their character and lineage. Before long, Abdul Muttalib's sons, Abu Talib, Abbas, and Hamza, set out to ask for Khadija's hand in marriage for their nephew. The proper ceremonies needed to be held among the families and then they would hold the wedding. First, Abu Talib began speaking, "All praise be to Allah, Who has made us from the lineage of Abraham and Ishmael! There is no doubt that He is the One Who made us to be of service to humanity, honored us with serving His House. Verily, He is the One Who made humankind turn towards His House, where people feel secure."

Then he said, "When it comes to my brother's son, Muhammad, he is the son of Abdullah. Whoever competes with him will certainly see that my nephew, Muhammad, comes out on top. Although he may not have financial means and property, he is above anyone else in terms of nobleness, bravery, intellect, and virtue. He asks for your daughter, Khadija's, hand in marriage."

After Abu Talib said what he had, Khadija's uncle, Amr ibn Asad, stood up and told Khadija's virtues with similar words. Then he said, "All praise be to Allah Who has made us superior to others in what you have mentioned! You shall be witnesses, on the honorable name that we both share; I hereby wed Khadija, daughter of Khuwaylid, to Muhammad, Abdullah's son."

The attendants from the leading people of Quraysh were witnesses, too. After the ceremony, they started celebrating. They slaughtered sheep and camels, and had a enormous feast. Khadija was now the world's happiest woman. Words could not describe her happiness. That day, they beat tambourines in Khadija's house and the ladies enjoyed the wedding among themselves.

Allah's Messenger was twenty-five years old and Khadija was forty years old. After staying in Abu Talib's house for a few days, they moved to a house purchased from Hakim ibn Hizam.

The Household

Allah's Messenger and Khadija were not alone in their house. The Prophet's nanny, Umm Ayman, Khadija's son Hind from her first marriage with Abu Hala, and Zayd ibn Haritha were also living in this house. Zayd was a former slave who had been freed after he was given to Allah's Messenger. When he was eight years old, some horsemen of the Banu Qayn took him away in a raid. Then he was brought to the Ukaz Fair, so that they could sell him as a slave. Hakim ibn Hizam purchased him for 400 silver coins. He took and brought Zayd directly to his aunt, Khadija's house. He gave him to her as a gift. When Allah's Messenger saw Zayd, he asked Khadija, "Who is this child?"

She answered, "He is Zayd, a slave from the tribe of Kalb. My nephew brought him to me as a gift."

Looking at Zayd, the Prophet said, "If he were mine, for sure, I would definitely free him."

Upon hearing this, Khadija said, "Then he is yours," and she granted him Zayd ibn Haritha.

Allah's Messenger freed him immediately. After a while, Zayd's relatives saw him when they visited Mecca for pilgrimage. They informed Zayd's father about what they say upon returning home. When he heard this news, he quickly found his way to Mecca and searched for him. But Zayd preferred to stay with Allah's Messenger, instead of going with his father back to his family. Allah's Messenger had adopted him that day and announced it to all Meccan people.

Allah's Messenger was financially in a very good condition after he married Khadija. But at the same time, he also looked after a big family. His uncle, Abu Talib's, condition wasn't as good as his, and so he took care of his family as well. He had difficulties maintaining his family due to the recent drought in Mecca. Allah's Messenger wanted to relieve his burden, so he went to his uncle, Abbas, who was one of the wealthiest men among the Hashimities.

He said, "O Uncle! You know that your brother, Abu Talib's, household is crowded. Let's go and talk to him. I will take one of his sons to look after and you take the rest of them. That way, we can support him."

Abbas liked this idea. Without hesitation, he said, "Of course, let's do it now."

The two stood up and went to Abu Talib's side. They asked him, "Until this hard drought and famine problem is over, we want to take the responsibility of your two sons and look after them, so we can reduce your burden."

Abu Talib was satisfied with the offer. "Aqil and Talib should stay with me. You can take the other two," he said.

Upon hearing his uncle's words, our Prophet took Ali ibn Abu Talib, and his uncle Abbas took Jafar home. Thus, Ali , may Allah be pleased with him, started to live with Allah's Messenger and Khadija in their house. From now on, the Prophet was a father and Khadija was a compassionate mother to Ali.

Unlike other rich people, Khadija did not leave the housework to servants and maidens. Instead, she took care of her husband's needs by herself. She was so devoted to him that she felt uncomfortable if anything bothered him in the least. When Allah's Messenger met an unpleasant situation, he immediately went home and found peace near Khadija. There was great sincerity and submission between them. This relationship attracted the attention of others and caused them to look at their life with admiration. They were living in a time period, when ignorance was at its peak. However, their life was very pure. Other people, with whom they had close relationships with, were people of moral and honesty.

The first fruit of this happy and peaceful home was a son. Allah's Messenger named his son Qasim, and the nickname, Abu'l-Qasim (Father of Qasim)' was given to the Prophet as a result. But Qasim passed away soon after he had just begun to walk. Three years later, their first daughter Zaynab was born. Allah's Messenger was around thirty years old. Feeling sad after their son's decease, the noble parents were happy with their daughter's birth. A year later, Ruqayyah was born. About three years after her birth, Umm Kulthum was born.

The Trustworthy One Is Coming

Our beloved Prophet had reached the age of thirty-five. The most important thing on the Meccan people's agenda, during that period, was the repair of the Ka'ba, the House of Allah. The walls of the Ka'ba had really worn down due to all the rain and flooding. What's more, when the cover of the Ka'ba was damaged in a fire, the Meccans finally decided to renovate this holy structure. They were going to tear the Ka'ba down to the foundation that Prophet Abraham, upon him be peace, had laid, and they were going to build it up anew. One section was given to every tribe and the walls were built up. At last, the time came for the Holy Black Stone sent down from Paradise to be put in its place. However, since every tribe wished to be privileged with such an honor, disagreements started to rise amongst them. Over the course of about 5 days, the disagreements rose to such an extent that blood was going to be shed for its sake. Meanwhile, Hudhayfa ibn al-Yaman, who was one of the eldest amongst them, pointed to the door of the Banu Shayba which opened into the Ka'ba, and said, "O the people of the Quraysh! Let the first person to walk through this door be the judge in this matter that you are unable to agree on."

All who were present, agreed to this, and they started to wait for the first person that would enter through the door of the Banu Shayba. Just then, they noticed that Muhammad the Trustworthy had entered through the door. His honesty and beautiful manners was always appreciated by all. They cried out in joy, "Behold, the Trustworthy One is coming! We are content with whatever He decides." When they told our Prophet of the situation, he said, "Bring me a covering."

He then placed the Holy Black Stone inside the big piece of cloth. He beckoned to a representative from each tribe and said to them, "Hold on to the covering, on behalf of your tribe! Then, all of you, lift up the cloth at the same time."

When the stone had been lifted to the point in which it would be placed, he embraced the Holy Black Stone and placed it in its rightful place with his own hands. Such judgment on his part had made everyone happy, and it had eliminated a great dispute that could have taken place. The honor of placing the Holy Stone that had been sent down from Paradise in the time of the first Prophet, Prophet Adam, had, in this way, been granted to the Last Prophet.

Divine Signs

A few years after the judging in the Ka'ba, our Prophet started to receive some signs from the Divine. This kept on for about 4 years. There was no doubt that the Divine light was starting to rise over Arabia. Sometimes he would hear voices calling out, "O Muhammad!" and other times there would be a series of flashing lights. His blessed wife, Khadija, was the only one that knew what was happening to him. Our blessed mother Khadija would give solace to him each time, and she would utter words of faith and confidence. She told him that Allah would never embarrass him. In fact, she had complete faith in the truth that her husband was the awaited last Prophet to come.

The scholars, who had long been in pursuit of the signs of the last Prophet, could also feel that his coming was very close. When the Messenger of Allah was thirty-eight years old, Ibn al-Hayyiban, a Jewish scholar, migrated to Medina. Before long, he had fallen sick while in Medina. When he realized that he was going to pass away, he called out to the Medinan Jews.

"O Jews! Do you know the true reason for my coming to this land of poverty and hunger, from a land abundant in food and drink?" he asked them.

When the Jews replied, "You know better than we do," Ibn al-Hayyiban said, "I came here to see the Prophet that would emigrate to this land! His time of coming is very close. O Jews! My advice to you is to be quick in joining him and following him, as I have done." Then, he passed away.

That same year, a famous scholar of his time, Quss ibn Saida, had read a sermon while atop his camel in the fair at Ukaz. In this sermon, which he read to a big crowd, he gave the good tidings that the time of the last Prophet's coming was drawing near. Those who were aware of what was written in the Holy Scriptures, their world was filled with these glad tidings during that period.

When the Messenger of Allah reached the age of thirty-nine he started having special, truthful dreams. Whatever he saw in his dreams at night, the same would happen during the day. This went on for about six months. Occasionally, he would hear the voice of a being that he could not see, calling out to him, saying, "O Muhammad!" As time went on, he had developed a liking to being alone by himself and had started to drift away from other people.

The fact that the society he was living in was leading an immoral life and that was suffocating him. Having forgotten the Creator of the universe, a majority of the people of Hijaz worshipped idols they made with their own hands, while others did not accept any belief at all. This worldly life was everything for them. All aspects of immorality, such as alcohol consumption, gambling, adultery, theft, fraud, and oppression had become a part of the daily life of society. The strong could very well force the weak into doing whatever they pleased. A person's life had no value in their eyes. Being sold into slavery in the bazaar after an unexpected raid was not something out of the ordinary.

There was another group that believed in Allah and the Hereafter, yet failed to accept the belief that a Prophet was going to emerge from amongst the people. There were others that accepted the existence of Allah but did not believe in life after death. Aside from all of these, you could also find very few people that lived according to the monotheistic religion of Prophet Abraham. The idol-worshippers had filled even the Ka'ba with their idols. Yet, the Ka'ba was the first building in this world built according to the orders of Allah in order to bring peace and serenity to the people.

Allah's Messenger could in no way break away from the Ka'ba, but the ways of the idol-worshipers was also hurting him deep within. Our Prophet witnessed these acts with a deep sadness; he wanted to ease the pain within and bring comfort to his soul. He had recently started to drift away from other people, wondering off to deserted areas, by himself, to ponder on his thoughts.

He would especially go up to the Mountain of Light very often. He would walk for hours to reach the mountain. He would sit inside the cave of Hira, facing the Ka'ba, and would dive deep in his gaze towards the Ka'ba. He had made it a habit to come to this cave on certain days of the year; this cave in which he would be alone with his Lord and would find peace and serenity.

Our Prophet found the cave of Hira very peaceful, yet each time he left home, Khadija would worry after him. She was frightened that something bad would happen to Allah's Messenger. So, she would send her men after him to make sure that he was safe and sound. She would constantly instruct her men to protect him from any possible danger. There were many times when Khadija herself also followed in his path towards the Mountain of Light. She would walk the long miles for hours and would climb the 860-meter-high Mountain of Light and would bring food to Allah's Messenger.

The bright light our Prophet saw around him and the voices that he heard had started to occur even more often than before. Especially as he left Mecca behind and came closer to the cave of Hira, he would hear voices say, "Peace be upon you, O Messenger of Allah!" He would immediately look to his right and left yet would see nothing else but the trees and rocks along the path. These things he experienced started making him anxious and worried. He would immediately come home and would tell his beloved wife, Khadija, of the things that happened to him. He would find comfort in her words.

On one of the days that he was returning from the cave of Hira, he heard someone calling out to him, saying,

"O Muhammad! I am the Archangel Gabriel!"

Allah's Messenger shuddered with anxiety; he went to Khadija's side and said to her, "I am worried that something bad will come to me."

With her soothing tone of voice Khadija said to him, "Don't utter such words! Allah will not embarrass such a servant as you! For you are a man who does not neglect that which is entrusted to you. You maintain your ties with those of your kin, you rush to their aid in their time of need, and you always tell the truth."

It was yet another night; the darkness had fallen and everyone had gone into their homes. A deep silence ruled all around him, and at that moment, our Prophet heard the Archangel Gabriel's voice once again. The voice said to him, "Peace be upon you."

Our Prophet walked towards his home in hurried steps. When Khadija noticed the flustered way about him, she asked, "What is the matter? Did something happen?"

As soon as our Prophet finished describing what had happened to him, she cried out in excitement, "How wonderful for you, because peaceful greetings can only signify good." The dreams he previously had, the glad tidings told of in the Holy Scriptures, and the things he was now experiencing, they all seemed to complement each other. These were the signs of Prophethood that had been longingly awaited for years.

Soon after, they went to Khadija's cousin, Waraqa ibn Nawfal, to tell him of the events that had been happening. Waraqa ibn Nawfal was not at all surprised with what he heard. Every Prophet told of in the Holy Scriptures had experienced such events. He turned to Allah's Messenger in a very calm manner, and said to him, "There is nothing harmful for you in this."

When our Prophet said, "When I hear that voice, I change my direction and walk away in fear," Waraqa responded, "Don't do such a thing! When the one who is calling out to you comes, be patient and listen to what he has to say to you! Then come to me and tell me of the things you heard."

It hadn't been long until one day our Prophet was alone by himself once again, and he heard a voice call out, "O Muhammad!" This time, when he heard the voice, he did not walk away but waited a while longer, just as Waraqa had told him to do. The voice said to him, "O Muhammad! Say, 'La ilaha illallah (There is no deity but Allah).'"

In the meantime, Allah's Messenger was still seeing the special signs in his dreams. One time, he had seen a hole being opened on the top of his house by removing a piece of wood on the rooftop, then a silver staircase had been placed and two men had entered the house through this hole. Upon this sight, he had wanted to call someone for help but had been unable to speak. Then, these two men sat on either side of him. One of them took hold of him, reached into his body and took out two of his rib bones. Then, the man reached for his heart, taking it out and giving it to his hand. Meanwhile, the man was saying to his friend, "What a beautiful heart this righteous man has."

Then he cleaned the heart and put it back into its rightful place. Before long, he also put the ribs back into their place. Afterwards, the men headed back in the direction they had come—they went up the stairs and disappeared out of sight. They took the staircase with them as they went. The roof was also retrieved to its previous state, and all was back to normal.

When our Prophet described his dream to Khadija, once again, she said, "Glad tidings to you!"

Then she continued, "There is no doubt that Allah only wants what is best and good for you. And that is wonderful tidings!"

What Should I Read?

The Master of the Universe was now forty years old. It was the month of Ramadan in the year 610. He had, once again, withdrawn himself into the cave of Hira and had dived deep into spiritual thoughts. Nowadays, he would be hearing the voice of the being which he could not see, more and more often. On the 17th night of Ramadan, after midnight, he heard a voice calling out to him by name. When he raised his head and looked around he saw that a blinding light covered every corner. Archangel Gabriel stood before him and said, "Read."

Our Prophet replied, "I do not know how to read!"

In response, the Archangel embraced Allah's Messenger with a strong hold and let him go. Once more, he said, "Read!"

Our Prophet replied, in the same way, "I do not know how to read!"

The Archangel embraced him with a strong hold again, and let him go, and said, "Read," one more time.

Our Prophet asked, "What should I read?"

Archangel Gabriel recited the first five verses of Surah al-Alaq: *"Read! Read in and with the Name of your Lord, Who has created! He created human from a clot clinging (to the wall of the womb). Read! Your Lord is the All-Munificent. Who has taught (human) by the pen, taught human what he did not know."*

And then, he left our Prophet's side and went away. The verses which the Archangel carried from his Lord had been inscribed onto our Prophet's heart line by line. Trembling over the things he experienced, our Prophet came out of the cave of Hira with excitement and started walking down the Mountain of Light. When he came about halfway down the mountain, he heard the voice from the skies once more. Archangel Gabriel was saying,

"O Muhammad! You are the Messenger of Allah! And I am the Archangel Gabriel!"

Our Prophet turned his head this way and that in order to avoid seeing the Archangel but saw him in every direction nevertheless! The voice of the Archangel of revelation was coming from all directions. When, at last, the Archangel Gabriel left his side, our Prophet returned to his home. He was terribly frightened and exhausted. He drew close to Khadija's side and said, "Cover me, cover me."

Noble Khadija laid him down on his bed and covered him at once. Our Prophet fell asleep with the shiver still in his heart. When he awoke he described everything that had happened to him, one by one, to Khadija. He said, "I am afraid that something bad will come to me."

With a voice full of compassion, Khadija put her hands on top of our Prophet's hands, and said, "Good tidings to you, o the son of my uncle! Persevere and be steadfast! I believe that you are the Prophet of this nation. Bear no doubt, Allah will surely protect you. For you give support to your relatives, you speak the truth, you hold the hands of the fallen and clothe those in need. You are always generous to guests, and you have devoted yourself completely to righteous ways."

Then, without wasting any time, they explained all that had happened to Waraqa ibn Nawfal. Waraqa was overjoyed. With shaky tone of voice he uttered these words,

"O Muhammad! I swear that you are the Prophet of this nation! The Archangel that came to you is the greatest Archangel of Allah, the Archangel Gabriel, and the Archangel that came to Prophet Moses before you. I wish I could live to see the day that your people will cast you out of your hometown, so that I could support you on that day."

Not being able to hide his astonishment to Waraqa's last words, our Prophet asked him,

"Are my people really going to cast me out of my hometown?" Waraqa replied, "Yes, they certainly will cast you out. For there is not a single person who has come with the Truth that you bear and has not been driven out of his homeland."

Then he approached our Prophet and kissed him on his forehead.

The First Believers

After the coming of the first Revelation, the revelations came to a standstill for forty days. However, our Prophet continued to frequently see Archangel Gabriel in different forms and hear his voice. Each time he saw the Archangel he would grow both afraid and exhausted. One day, as he came out of the cave of Hira and walked down the Mountain of Light, he heard the voice of the Archangel of revelation. When he lifted his head up to look, he saw Archangel Gabriel in the skies. He returned to his home, full of fear and excitement, and asked Khadija to cover him. However, right at that same time, Archangel Gabriel brought the first verses of Surah al-Muddathir: *"O, you cloaked one (who has preferred solitude)! Arise and warn! And declare your Lord's (indescribable and incomparable) greatness! And keep your clothing clean. Keep away from all material and spiritual impurities..."* Henceforth, the Revelation was not intermitted until the Holy Qur'an was completed. The verses continued to be revealed throughout different time periods.

The duty of Prophethood had thus been granted to the Messenger. The Messenger of Allah then turned to his blessed wife, Khadija and said, "O Khadija! From now on, the time for sleep and comfort is over. The Archangel Gabriel ordered me to warn people and invite them to believe in Allah. Who shall I invite, who will answer my call?" In response, Khadija declared, "Glad tidings be to you! I swear to Allah, He has not willed anything but goodness for you. What comes to you from Allah is real and is the Truth. I am the first of those you have invited and I am the first to answer your call."

In this way, she became the first to believe in the Messenger of Allah and those that were revealed to him from Allah.

It hadn't been very long until, one day, the Messenger of Allah was standing atop a high hill near Mecca and the Archangel Gabriel appeared at once before him. This time, the Archangel of Revelation had become visible to the noble Prophet in the form of a human being. He approached our Prophet and hit the ground with his heel. Water started gushing out of the spot that he had struck. Then he made *wudu* (ablutions) in front of our Prophet. And our Prophet repeated the steps after him. After that, the Archangel taught our Prophet how he was to perform the Daily Prayer. And, again, our Prophet repeated the steps after him. When the Archangel Gabriel went away, the Messenger of Allah returned to his home. He taught everything that he had learned from the Archangel Gabriel one by one to Khadija and together they made *wudu* and performed the Prayers. In this way, Khadija became once more the first person in the religion of Islam to make *wudu*, perform the Prayers and stand behind our Prophet in Prayer.

Ali ibn Abu Talib had seen the Messenger of Allah and Khadija praying together, and he had watched the curiously for a while. He was only ten years old at the time. He approached the Messenger of Allah and asked him what they were doing. Our Prophet sat Ali on his knee and told him, one by one, everything that had happened to him in the cave of Hira. With a voice full of compassion he said to Ali, "He is the One and only Allah. He has no partners. He has created all beings and provides their sustenance. It is He who creates life and death. He is the All-Powerful."

Ali both trusted and loved our Prophet very much. However, this was an important decision, so he felt the need to consult his father. The Messenger of Allah said to him, "O Ali! If you are willing to do what I tell you, then do it! Otherwise, keep this as a secret between us."

Ali wasn't able to sleep at all that night. He thought over and over about what our Prophet had told him. And, in the end, he decided not to ask his father about this matter. As soon as morning came, he went to Allah's Messenger and asked him, "What was it that you talked to me about yesterday?"

A smile spread over our Prophet's face. The Messenger of Allah told Ali to sit next to him and invited him to declare the *Shahada*, or testimony of faith. Thus, little Ali, who was only ten years old then, had been honored by being the first person after Khadija to declare the Oneness and Unity of Allah.

In those first days, the Prayers were performed twice a day, in the morning and evening, and in the form of two *rakah*s, or units. The Messenger of Allah would search for a calm place to perform his Prayers and would, most of the time, go out of Mecca for this. Ali ibn Abu Talib would secretly follow him. They would pray together amongst the date trees and would return home when it was nighttime. On one such day, Abu Talib passed from a nearby distance while on his way. The movements that his son and nephew were making drew his attention. When it was nighttime and they had returned, he went to them and asked, "O my brother's son! What is this religion of yours?" And our Prophet replied, "O my uncle! This is the religion of Allah! This is the religion of Allah's Archangels. This is the religion of the Messengers of Allah. This is the religion of our forefather, Abraham. Allah has chosen me and sent me as a Prophet to all of humanity. My uncle! You are most worthy of this invitation and of helping me in this cause."

Abu Talib paused for a while, looked with compassion at his beloved nephew and said to him, "O my brother's son! I cannot abandon the religion of my forefathers! But, let this be my oath before Allah, that I will be by your side as long as I live. While you are pursuing this cause, whenever you encounter something that makes you unpleasant, I will be at your aid."

He then turned to his son, Ali, and asked him, "O my son! "What happened to you? What is this new state that I see you in?" Ali answered with excitement, "I have put my faith in Allah and His Messenger. I have also affirmed everything else that comes with him. I pray with him, and from now on, I will always be behind him, never to leave his side."

Abu Talib did not have any objections to what he heard. "He will only invite you to do good. Follow in his path," he said, and then he turned around and walked away.

Abu Talib's words had made both our Prophet and Ali very happy. Soon after, Zayd ibn Haritha, who also lived in the Prophet's home, became a Muslim as well and joined those that had been honored with the blessing of faith. During that time, our Prophet's closest friend, Abu Bakr, was also returning to Mecca from Yemen, where he had gone for trade. As he reached Mecca he saw that some of the Qurayshi leaders were waiting for him to arrive. He asked them, "What happened here while I was away? What is the latest new? Is there anything new?"

They had been waiting for this question all along. They began explaining, with hatred and contempt, "O Abu Bakr, what incredible news! Abu Talib's orphan believes that he is a Prophet. If it weren't for you, we would have finished him off by now. However, since you are here now, we are certain that you will find a solution."

They were certain that Abu Bakr would solve the situation, so they told him of the events over and over again. Abu Bakr was not listening to them anymore. He was lost in his thoughts of the past. He remembered one by one the dream that he had had twenty years ago in Damascus and also remembered the Christian priest Bahira's interpretation of his dream. When he was only eighteen years old, he had gone to Damascus for trade and had had a very interesting dream on one of the nights that he spent there. In his dream, the moon had fallen over the city of Mecca and a piece of the moon had entered every home in the city. Then, all of these pieces had gathered in Abu Bakr's home. Abu Bakr was not able to shake off the influence the dream had over him for a long time and on his way back to Mecca he had spent the night in Busra and had asked priest Bahira to interpret his dream. In his interpretation, the priest had spoken of the last Prophet that was to come. He had told Abu Bakr that the time of his coming was very close and that he was going to be the most fortunate person that would help the Prophet throughout his life.

Abu Bakr thought of the good tidings that had been spoken of for years, tidings of a last Prophet to come. He remembered the words of Zayd ibn Amr about a long missed Prophet that he had listened to in the courtyard of the Ka'ba. He remembered the advice of Quss ibn Saida, the old dervish of the fairs. So, this was it. For years they had been waiting for this time, and it had finally come. Muhammad, the Trustworthy One's duty had been conveyed to him and Abu Bakr's dream had come true.

Without losing any time, Abu Bakr went straight towards Khadija's home. He was going to speak to Muhammad, the Trustworthy. As he was quickly walking down the road, he saw that our Prophet was coming towards him. He grew excited. Apparently both had set out to find the other. Abu Bakr asked, "O Muhammad! Is it true that you have rejected the religion of our forefathers?" Without any hesitation, the Messenger of Allah replied, "Yes, surely, I am the servant and Messenger of Allah. O Abu Bakr! I invite you to believe in the one and only Allah."

Upon this, Abu Bakr asked, "What have you to prove that this is true?"

The Messenger of Allah replied, "The dream which you saw and had Bahira interpret years ago." When Abu Bakr said, "I swear to Allah that I believe in everything that you have said, reach out your hand to me," without the slightest hesitation, our Prophet reached his hand towards Abu Bakr.

Abu Bakr put his hand over our Prophet's hand and said, "I testify that there is no deity but Allah and that Muhammad is His servant and Messenger." He was now a Muslim.

Prophet Muhammad: The Seal of All Prophets

News of Abu Bakr becoming a Muslim had spread all over Mecca and had completely shocked everyone. The unbelievers were disappointed and did not like this news one bit. Abu Bakr, on the other hand, announced his new faith, without reserve, and started inviting the people to believe in Allah the Almighty and His Messenger. He worked with zeal and diligence to share the beauty that he experienced so that others could be honored with the blessing of faith as well.

The Secret Invitation

Following Khadija, Zayd ibn Haritha, Ali ibn Abu Talib, and Abu Bakr; Uthman ibn Affan, Abdu'r-Rahman ibn Awf, Sa'd ibn Abi Waqqas, Zubayr ibn al-Awwam, and Talha ibn Ubaydullah , may Allah be pleased with them, had also chosen Islam and had become a part of the first Muslims. From that point on, the period of secret invitation, which was to last for three years, had started. Conveying the Divine message was yet through personal efforts within a small circle. The number of people that believed in Allah and His Messenger was increasing one by one. New verses of the Qur'an were being conveyed to the Messenger of Allah, and he shared these with the first Muslims around him. For this they would mostly come together in quiet and secluded places. Most of the time, it would be our Prophet's home that they gathered in for these meetings. In this way, they were trying to avoid any negative reaction from the Quraysh tribe.

The polytheists, who had been associating partners with Allah for years, through idols that they had been making with their own hands, were truly unhappy about these recent developments. They had no intention of abandoning the religion of their ancestors and accepting the Oneness of Allah and the Prophethood of Allah's Messenger instead. During the first years of Islam, they had preferred to merely watch and observe the advancement of this newly emerging religion. They thought that it would be just a temporary phase. The polytheists simply made fun of whatever they heard, and they kept on denying the Messenger of Allah. Contrary to their expectations, this was certainly not the case. As days passed, the people started running towards the true religion and were enlightened by faith, one by one.

Among these first people to be honored with Islam were some of the close relatives of the Messenger of Allah. However, so far, not even one of his four uncles had decided to follow him. Abu Talib hadn't objected to his sons, Jafar and Ali, embracing Islam yet he himself had refused to abandon the religion of his ancestors. Although his uncles, Abbas and Hamza loved the Messenger of Allah dearly, they just could not decide whether or not to choose Islam as a religion. Abu Lahab, on the other hand, explicitly accused his nephew of dishonesty and claimed that by turning away from the religion of their ancestors, he was making a very big mistake.

During this period of secret invitation to Islam, the number of people who embraced Islam was not more than thirty. Believers worshipped in their own homes and secretly read the newest revelations of the Qur'an. Most of the time, they met in quiet, secluded places outside Mecca to perform Prayer in congregation.

One day, some individuals from the Quraysh, saw the Muslims while in Prayer and made fun of this sight they had never before witnessed. A conflict rose between the two sides and Sa'd ibn Abi Waqqas one of the Companions of our Prophet, hit one of the non-believers with the rib bone of a camel and wounded him. This was the first spill of blood in the name of Islam. After that day, however, they decided to stay away from any form of violence because the Revelation constantly advised the Muslims to be patient.

Allah's Messenger's saddened heart would find tranquility and serenity in his home. Our Prophet's blessed wife Khadija would ease his sadness with her comforting words and would do her best to make his duty easier on him. During that first year of calling to the true religion, Islam, one of the events that brought joy into the Prophet's home had been the birth of their daughter, Fatima. The Messenger of Allah announced the glad news of his daughter's birth by saying, "Just now, the Archangel of revelation came and congratulated us for this new child that came into the world. Allah has given her the name Fatima."

Warn Your Relatives

When the verse *"(O Messenger) warn your nearest kinsfolk"* (ash-Shu'ara 26:214) was revealed to the Messenger of Allah during the fourth year of his Prophethood, the Messenger of Allah beckoned to Ali and asked him to invite all his relatives to Abu Talib's home and to prepare a feast of mutton and milk for them. Ali did as he was told and gathered all their relatives. The plate of food and the bowl of milk put before the guests was only enough to feed a single person. Our Prophet started first by saying, "In the Name of Allah," then said, "Help yourself!" to all their relatives. Though the guests were a total of forty people, the meal for one person had been enough to feed them all. Through our Prophet's miracle of abundance and bounty the meal hadn't decreased one bit and all who came were amazed. After the meal, as the Messenger of Allah was getting ready to start speaking about his invitation to his relatives to embrace Islam, Abu Lahab spoke out. "This is absolutely astonishing! I see that this man has bewitched you," he said. The he turned to our Prophet, said, "I have never seen another man that has brought such evil to their relatives as you have," and continued with his insulting words.

The tension in the room was really starting to build up. Upon this, the guests all departed before the Messenger of Allah could say anything. A short while after this incident, our Prophet organized a second meeting and, this time, after the feast, he stood up and said,

"O the sons of Abdul Muttalib! All praise and thanks are to Allah. I believe in Him, I hold on to Him. Only from Him do I ask for help. Surely, there is no deity but Allah. He is One. None is comparable to Him; He does not have any partners! I swear to Allah that you will, one day, die as though you are falling asleep. You will be brought back to life as though you are awakening from your sleep and you will be judged for all that you have done! You will be rewarded for the good that you have done, and you will be punished for the evil that you have committed! And, in the end, you will either stay forever in Paradise or in Hell! You are the first people that I am warning! I invite you to accept that there is no deity other than Allah and that I am His servant and Messenger. Who will accept being my brother and supporter, who will accept being rewarded with the gardens of Paradise?"

All who were there stood in astonishment. Not a single sound could be heard.

Though he could be considered a child at the time, it was Ali's strong voice that broke the silence, "I will, O Messenger of Allah! I will support you in this cause."

The Messenger of Allah was moved by this very sincere attitude; he caressed Ali's head and said, "Behold! He is my brother and my closest supporter. Listen to him and heed what he is telling you."

Some of the guests stood up laughing and said to Abu Talib, "See! Muhammad is ordering you to listen to your son! Why don't you obey him?"

However, Abu Talib responded with a tone of voice that made it obvious that he did not appreciate their attitude.

"Muhammad will not guide him to anything but goodness," he said. Then he turned to our Prophet, saying, "I will always be by your side. I will never refrain from protecting you. You go on with your call to Islam."

Right then and there, Safiyya, one of our Prophet's aunts, declared her belief in Allah, without any hesitation whatsoever. His other aunts, however, were not able to decide on it yet, but, nevertheless, they spoke in a gentle manner. When our Prophet's uncle, Abu Lahab, started saying unpleasant things like, "O the sons of Abdul Muttalib! I swear to Allah that this is mischief and malice! Stop him before others do," our Prophet's aunt, Safiyya, rebuked him and said, "O my brother! Is it appropriate for you to despise and hold your nephew and his religion in contempt? Why are you still behaving this way, even though you are aware of the fact that scholars have informed us of a Prophet arising from Abdul Muttalib's descent?"

Abu Lahab went on with his heinous speech in spite of his sister, and, this time, Abu Talib, who was getting angry with Abu Lahab, said, "You coward! I swear to Allah that we will help and protect him as long as we live." And he turned to our Prophet and said, "O my brother's son! Let us know of the times you wish to call people to believe in their Lord, and we shall take up arms and come forward with you."

And so, they all separated and went on their ways.

Openly Conveying the Message

In the following days, the Messenger of Allah continued his call to the true religion. While some people insisted on denying everything, others complied with his calling and became enlightened with the faith. Upon the revelation of the new verses that read, *"So from now on, proclaim what you are commanded to convey openly and in an emphatic manner, and do not care (whatever) those who associate partners with Allah (say and do). We suffice you against all those who mock"* (al-Hijr 94–95), which Archangel Gabriel had brought, our Prophet stood on top of the Safa Hill, and shouted, "O the people of Quraysh!" All who heard the news, "Muhammad is calling out from on top of Safa Hill!" gathered around him. Full of curiosity, they called out, "O Muhammad! What is the matter?"

In response, the Messenger of Allah asked, "If I were to inform you that enemy warriors were about to fall upon you from behind that hill, would you believe me?"

"Yes! We would believe you! For we know you never lie and you are the one of great honesty," they replied.

Our Prophet had found the answer he was hoping for. Afterwards, he called out, "O the sons of Fihr! O the sons of Abdul Muttalib!" and mentioned the names of all the families of the Quraysh tribe, and he said to them, "I have been entrusted with a duty to warn you. Come and protect yourself

Prophet Muhammad: The Seal of All Prophets

from the Hell-fire. I invite you to embrace faith by declaring 'Allah is One and there is no deity but Allah.' Until you say, 'La ilaha illallah (There is no deity but Allah)' I cannot be of any help to you either in this world or in the next."

As soon as the Messenger of Allah finished his words, his uncle, Abu Lahab, who was also among the crowd, picked up a stone and shouted, "Shame on you! Is this what you gathered us all here for?"

Then, he threw that stone in his hand at our Prophet. Our Prophet, however, continued with his call, saying, "O the people of the Quraysh! Save yourselves from the punishment of Hell! I have nothing to protect you from the punishment of Allah!"

No one else in the crowd behaved in the way Abu Lahab did, but they did not accept what they had heard just now, either. They just talked among themselves and went on their ways. Upon the rejection and enmity of Abu Lahab, Surah al-Masad, which begins with the verses, *May both hands of Abu Lahab be ruined, and ruined are they!*" (al-Masad 111:1) was revealed by Allah.

After this open invitation to Islam on Safa Hill, everyone in Mecca had heard about Islam. The Messenger of Allah, who had been inviting the sons of Abdul Muttalib to Allah at every chance, had started to gradually extend his circle of invitation to Islam. From that point on, he would go to the Ka'ba without hiding, perform Prayers there, openly call people to Islam, and freely read the Qur'an. Just like the Prophets that had come before him, he said, "O my tribe! Come and be a servant to the One Allah Who has no equal."

The Plans of the Non-believers

The Meccan polytheists, who were living in a state of darkness and ignorance, and who had no intention of stopping their worship of idols, at first remained indifferent to the invitation to Islam. However, in time, some of them started to show an explicit enmity towards Islam. The unbelievers realized that with Islam, which commands people to stop their wrongdoings and misbehavior, they would be rather restricted. Therefore, their anger and enmity towards Allah's Messenger grew more and more. In the meantime, the hajj season was coming. Arabs from all around Arabia were going to come to Mecca and they would hear about our Prophet's invitation. This time, the polytheists of the Quraysh started to think about how they would act against this situation.

According to them, most of the Arabs coming to Mecca during hajj time would never come back to Mecca after hearing the latest news. This would, in turn, both negatively affect their trade business and alter the image and respectability of the Meccans. Even worse, there was a possibility that the Arabs would all come together and banish the people of Quraysh from the Ka'ba. This would mean that Mecca would be handed over to the control of a different tribe. The situation was quite serious. For this reason, the non-believers immediately came together and formed a consultative committee, and they started talking about what actions they could take against this.

In the end, they decided to give the Arabs pilgrims and traders coming into Mecca the message that the Messenger of Allah did not represent the people of Quraysh. The easiest way to do this was to tell everyone that he was not a Prophet. However, there had to be other things they could tell them. Some of them found it convenient to call him crazy while others decided to describe him as soothsayer, poet, or magician. According to Walid ibn Mughira, one of the leading non-believers, our Prophet possessed the power to separate the believers from their brothers, spouses, and even their whole family. Walid claimed that even though Muhammad was not a true sorcerer, he shared many commonalities with them. Actually, all of them knew very well that Muhammad, the Trustworthy, was neither poet nor a sorcerer. They even admitted it to each other from time to time; yet they did not give up on their rejection and were persistent in their ignorance.

In the end, the polytheists of the Quraysh decided to wait at the entrance points to Mecca to warn those coming into the city for the hajj. Before giving them the opportunity to meet with the Messenger of Allah, they intended to tell them that there was a man named Muhammad who brought about a new religion and totally disregarded all their idols. And, in this way, they intended to interfere with the invitation of the Messenger of Allah. They did just what they had planned to do. Regardless of all they tried to do, our Prophet did not stop informing people about the revelations of Allah.

The Listeners of the Qur'an

On one hand, during the daytime, our beloved Prophet would endure all these troubles, and on the other hand, when everybody was sound asleep, he would go to the Ka'ba and would perform his Prayers and supplications there. The nights in our Prophet's home were an especially beautiful experience. With his beautiful voice, the Messenger of Allah would recite out loud the verses that had been revealed to him. Most Meccans, who knew that he recited the Qur'an at nights, couldn't stop themselves from secretly coming to his home and listening to the Qur'an, even if they did not believe in him. Those who listened to him even once, wished to listen to him over and over again. Some leaders of the non-believers, Abu Jahl and Ahnas, were also among those who secretly listened to the Qur'an. These people who couldn't bring themselves to admit they listened to the Qur'an, would secretly come out of their homes at night and would come to our Prophet's home doing their best to not be seen by anyone. They would listen to the Divine words from different corners of our Prophet's home, completely unaware of each other. On some nights, they would run into each other on their way back home, but they would act as though they hadn't seen each other and would quietly be on their way. No matter how captivating the words they listened to were, still, these enemies of Islam did not accept the faith. Carried away with their *nafs*, or ego, they deemed themselves superior; in the event that they accept the faith, they feared that the other non-believers would ridicule them. Such were the futile thoughts that they were dragged into. What's more, by forbidding all from listening to the Qur'an they wanted to prevent the people from drawing closer to the faith.

However, no matter what the enemies of Islam tried to do, the Muslims did not, for a second, give up on reading the Qur'an and speaking of their faith. During this period of calling to faith, one night, Umar ibn al-Khattab, who happened to be present at the time, listened to our Prophet recite Surah al-Haqqah while in the Ka'ba. One of the prominent leaders of Mecca, Umar ibn al-Khattab was a great warrior and was a fearless and brave man. He also was one of the people who lived according to the customs of the Period of Ignorance, or Jahiliyya, and he found our Prophet's calling meaningless. He sat at a corner and started listening to the verses. He was greatly moved by the verses that our Prophet recited from the Qur'an. He couldn't stop himself from being amazed by the Divine words that he heard, and thought, "Yes, the rumors must be true. He is certainly an impressive poet, like my friends have said. The extraordinarily beautiful sentences can only flow from the lips of a poet. "Just then, the Messenger of Allah was reciting the 40th and 41st verses: *"It surely is the speech (conveyed to you by) an illustrious, noble Messenger, and not a poet's speech (composed in a poet's mind). How little is what you believe! (It is so limited by the poverty of your souls and hearts)."*

Umar ibn al-Khattab was startled. For the Messenger of Allah had, in that very instant, responded to what he had been thinking just now. "All right; because he can read what's in my mind, then he must be a fortune-teller," he thought to himself. Our Prophet continued to recite, *"Nor is it a sooth-sayer's speech (pretending to foretell events). How little it is that you reflect and be mindful! (It is so limited by the poverty of your minds). (No indeed!) It is a Revelation being sent down in parts from the Lord of the worlds. If he (the Messenger) had dared to fabricate some false sayings in attribution to Us, We would certainly have seized him with might; Thereafter, We would certainly have cut his life-vein. Then not one from among you could have shielded and saved him from Us. And it is a sure Reminder (bringing hope and guidance) for the Allah-revering, pious. We are most certainly aware that among you are some who deny (it). It will surely be a bitter regret for the unbelievers. And this (the whole Qur'an) is surely certain truth. So glorify the Name of your Lord, the Supreme."*

Umar ibn al-Khattab was overwhelmed with emotion. He couldn't stop his tears from pouring down. All of a sudden, he recalled the idols that he worshipped. How could he have neglected them! How could he give up on the religion that had been a part of him for years?

He had to free himself from the influence of the words he had been listening to. Thus, he took off from where he was, right away. Even though he had come so close to the truth, he dragged himself back into the darkness of unbelief once again. Nevertheless, the beautiful words that he had overheard kept on ringing in his ears. He had listened to many poets before but had never heard such things from any one of them.

The Complaint to Abu Talib

Advances in the spreading of Islam were exasperating and nerve wracking for the non-believers. They tried every possible method but were unsuccessful in dissuading or deterring even a single person from their faith. Nonetheless, no matter what it took, this calling had to be brought to an end. In the end, the non-believers decided to ask his uncle, Abu Talib, to stop our Prophet. Abu Talib was the leader of the Hashimites. They went to him and told him that he needed to talk his nephew out of this calling, this mission that he was after. Abu Talib listened to what they had to say and responded to them in a peaceful and conciliatory manner. The Qurayshi non-believers waited for a period of time, but after seeing that there was no change in our Prophet's behavior, they went to Abu Talib once more, and said to him,

"O Abu Talib, you are a very important man for us. We asked you to stop your brother's son. Yet you failed to do what was necessary. Let this be a vow that we will neither endure our ancestors being looked at as lowly nor our gods being ridiculed. Stop him, or else we will make war with both you and him until one of the two sides perishes. If he is to give up on this calling, we promise to give him whatever he pleases. If he desires wealth, we will give him wealth. If he desires to reign, we will make him our emperor. Whatever else it is that he desires, we shall give it to him. So long as he gives up on this mission.

Upon this, Abu Talib came to our Prophet and let him know of what he had been told. He continued, "O my brother's son, protect yourself and me both. Don't make me take on more than I can carry."

Hearing such words from his uncle had hurt our Prophet so. His eyes had filled with tears. He looked at his uncle and said, "O my uncle! I swear to Allah that even if you put the sun in my right hand, and the moon in my left, I will never give up in my calling! Either Allah will spread His religion all throughout the world or I will give up my life for this very cause."

As our Prophet, who had been deeply saddened, slowly got up to leave, his uncle Abu Talib called him back to his side and reassured him, saying, "O my brother's son, go and do as you like. I swear to Allah, I will never leave you, and I will never, for whatever reason, hand you over to anyone."

The Increasing Tyranny

The non-believers had finally understood that Abu Talib would keep on protecting his nephew and would not desert him, no matter what. On the other hand, they were constantly making all kinds of insidious plans to harm the Messenger of Allah and his biggest supporter, Khadija. For this reason, their sons-in-law were under great pressure to divorce the three daughters, whom they had married before the coming of the revelations. Their oldest daughter, Zaynab, was married to Khadija's sister, Hala's son, Abu al-As. And they had married their two daughters, Ruqayyah and Umm Kulthum, to Abu Lahab's two sons, Utba and Utayba.

The Qurayshi non-believers guaranteed the Messenger of Allah's sons-in-law that if they were to divorce our Prophet's daughters, they could wed any other girl they pleased in the land. Our Prophet's uncle Abu Lahab, being the father-in-law of both, was among the first to advise so. After the revelation of Surah al-Masad, Abu Lahab's wife Umm Jamil talked to her two sons, Utba and Utayba, saying, "Ruqayyah and Umm Kulthum have rejected the religion of their forefathers. You must divorce them, you must leave them." Abu Lahab also talked to his two sons.

"If you do not divorce Muhammad's daughters, may my head become forbidden to you," he swore.

Upon hearing this, Utba and Utayba agreed to divorce our Prophet's daughters. The fact that their children's families were being torn apart deeply saddened our Prophet and our noble mother Khadija. What's more, there were no misdoings on their daughters' part. The only reason was that they were both the daughters of the Messenger of Allah. Abu Lahab and his wife Umm Jamil were overjoyed that they had hurt the Messenger's family by separating their sons from our Prophet's daughters. Their joy, however, was only able to last until Ruqayyah got married to Uthman ibn Affan, one of the richest men in Mecca.

Contrary to what they were hoping for, this separation had brought much more goodness for the Messenger's daughters. These new developments made the Qurayshi non-believers even more irritable and vicious. Not being able to tolerate the situation one bit, Abu Lahab started attacking the Messenger of Allah and his family even more. Not long after, he rose, one day, with fury and went directly to our Prophet's daughter Zaynab's husband Abu al-As.

"Leave your wife. We will wed you to whichever girl you desire in all the land," he said to him.

Abu al-As was furious at these words. He turned to Abu Lahab with anger and scolded him saying, "No, I swear to Allah that I will not leave my wife. I do not desire any other girl from the Quraysh in place of my wife."

Powerless to do anything, Abu Lahab returned to his home.

Saddened by this oppression, the Messenger of Allah sorrow deepened with a recent death. Abdullah, our Prophet's second son who had been born after the coming of Prophethood, had gone on to Paradise just as his big brother Qasim had. Our beloved Prophet was very upset and full of grief. This was the second time he was going through the loss of a child. The non-believers were ruthless enough to use even this time of grief to their advantage and against our Prophet. To make matters worse, the person taking the lead in these heinous plans was none other than the Messenger's very own uncle, Abu Lahab. In the morning right after the night of Abdullah's death, Abu Lahab had rushed amongst the Quraysh crying out at the top of his lungs, "Last night, Muhammad's progeny was cut off and brought to an end." He had not failed to use the death of a little child as a means to attack the Messenger of Allah. Uqba, Ka'b, and As were also among this caravan of non-believers that ridiculed our Prophet. They talked of how Allah's Messenger had no male children left and thus how his progeny was bound to dry up.

On one of these days, on his way back from visiting the Ka'ba, the Messenger of Allah ran into As, one of the Qurayshi non-believers, and stopped to talk to him for a while on the road. Later on, As joined the Qurayshi leaders, who were seating near the Ka'ba. They asked him,

"Who was it that you were talking to on the road?" His reply was, "I was talking to that 'abtar' man whose future generation is bound to go extinct! Leave him be! His sons have died, and his posterity has been cut off! His male children cannot live on. As time goes on, his name and reputation will not be heard of anymore. Then you will not have to worry about him anymore."

As he finished his words, they laughed heartily amongst each other. Before long, however, Allah the Almighty sent

Surah al-Kawthar to His Messenger. The verses explained that if there was anyone whose posterity would be cut off in this world, it would be those who showed enmity against the Messenger of Allah. As a matter of fact, Allah the Almighty actually did cut off the lineage of those who described our Prophet's posterity as such. And He made our Prophet's descent the greatest of all.

From Insult to Torture

Despite all their oppression and efforts, when the non-believers were not able to achieve what they hoped for in preventing the spread of Islam they decided to increase their tyranny even more. This time they intended to harm the Messenger of Allah himself. Abu Jahl, the commander of the non-believers, said to the others, "Tomorrow I will pick up a great big stone in my hand, and I will drop it on his head while he is prostrating in his Prayer." The others replied, "Do whatever you like, and we will support you."

The next day, our Prophet came to the Ka'ba to pray. Abu Jahl, who was holding a great big rock in his hands, approached our Prophet as he bent down in prostration. Then, all of a sudden, he drew back and fled away. He was trembling with fear and the rock had long dropped from his hands and crumbled. The non-believer watched with curiosity and later asked Abu Jahl what had happened then.

"A giant camel, at a size I had never before witnessed, was running at me. If I were to take a few steps forward, it was ready to devour me. So I fled," he narrated.

After witnessing such miracles some accepted the faith while others persisted in their denial. Despite everything else, the Messenger of Allah continued in his calling and, with every passing day, the number of believers kept on increasing.

What had started as mere ridicule by the Qurayshi non-believers had now turned into a form of insulting and torture. They were just not able to overcome their ignorance and become honored with a new faith.

They were not able to harm the Muslims that were from the prominent tribes of Mecca. On the other hand, though, they gave a really hard time to the believers who were poor and forlorn. They carried out every possible form of oppression and torture that they could think of in order to make the believers give up on their faith and also to prevent any more people from accepting the new faith.

Those tyrannizing and torturing the believers were leading Qurayshi non-believers like Abu Jahl, Abu Lahab, As, Umayya, Walid and Nadr. They did not hesitate one bit as they left the believers in hunger and thirst, imprisoned them, beat them until they fainted, crushed them underneath great rocks and left them to burn under the scorching sun.

Abu Bakr led the struggle in protecting the believers who were being oppressed. He freed seven slaves, including Bilal al-Habashi, who were Muslims, by paying an amount many times more than what their masters expected. He had wanted to free other slaves as well, but, no matter how high a price he offered, their masters had refused to grant them their freedom. They preferred to enjoy themselves by continuing to torture their Muslim slaves.

When Abu Jahl and his Companions decided to torture the forlorn Muslims, they first went to Ammar and his family. Ammar had become Muslim alongside his mother, Sumayya, and his father, Yasir. They were slaves belonging to the Banu Makhzum. The leaders of the tribe, with Abu Jahl as their head, would take them onto an open field during the hottest time of day and would torture them until they grew tired. The father, Yasir, a very old man, could not endure the torture much longer and, thus, continued on his journey towards Paradise. When Sumayya refused to reject her Lord and speak against the Messenger of Allah despite all the torture they were put through, she too was martyred through a last blow from Abu Jahl's spear. The worst part was that all this was happening right in front of Ammar's eyes. The non-believers had put him through so much spiritual and physical pressure and torture that Ammar had lost consciousness and was unaware of the things he spoke. The non-believers demanded furiously, "We will never let you go unless you speak well of Lat and Uzza!"

And, truly, it was only after he uttered their names that they let him go. Ammar had been set free but, spiritually, he was in deep pain. For, instead of speaking of Allah and His Messenger, both of whom he loved dearly and regarded above all else, he had dirtied his tongue by mentioning the names of those lifeless idols. He was completely worn out. He came to our Prophet's side, broken and torn down. He was ashamed beyond words. Before long, signs of the coming of a revelation became apparent in our Prophet. The revelation explained that when under torture and violence, the words that the believers were forced to speak would not be considered disbelief as long as their hearts did not affirm to it. Upon this, Ammar breathed a sigh of relief and went away with serenity in his heart.

The House of Arqam

As the non-believers increased their oppression and tyranny, our Prophet started in search of a place where it would be safer for them to continue their service of invitation to Allah. Finally he moved into a house in between the mountains, Safa and Marwa. The house belonged to Arqam, one of the Companions of our Prophet. Arqam's house was a part of the land in which Ka'ba was located, a land which was under Divine protection. The house was located on the northern side of Mount Safa, a very suitable location for coming in, going out, and keeping an eye on whose coming. Because the surroundings were crowded, it was hard for others to make out who went in and out of the house. The location of the house was also very convenient for the people to come together easily.

From then on, the Messenger of Allah came together with his Companions in this house, and spoke of Islam here. They would read the Qur'an together and pray together. Many Meccans became Muslim in this very house, which was called Dar'ul-Islam. Mus'ab ibn Umayr, the son of a noble family, was also among the ones who embraced faith in that house. Mus'ab came from a very wealthy and noble family. Both his mother and father spoiled him, tending to his every wish. He was a handsome and well-groomed young man. He was deeply reputable; it was considered an honor to be in his presence and he was highly respected. One day, overwhelmed by his curiosity about this new religion, he had gone to Arqam's house, and there he had recited the *Shahada*, declaring the Oneness of Allah and accepting Muhammad as His Messenger. Honored with the blessing of faith, Mus'ab's heart was filled with excitement. He was greatly angered by the non-believers denying our Prophet. However, due to the grave oppression and tyranny towards the believers during that period, he had to hide the truth, even from his family. He secretly came to visit our Prophet. When one of their neighbors saw him while praying one day and told of this to his family, all his relatives gathered around him. Mus'ab wished to tell them of this new religion he had embraced, and so, he stood up to read from the Qur'an. His mother raised up to silence him with a hard slap on the face but Mus'ab's reverent posture and serenity was enough to make her lower her hand. Nevertheless, she was convinced that it was her duty to take the revenge of the wooden and stone gods that her son had abandoned. She immediately confined him to a room. Days of trial and tribulation were just starting for this wealthy yet delicate young man of Mecca.

The Emigration to Abyssinia

The oppression and suffering was increasing, and so the Muslims started asking our Prophet for permission to immigrate to a place where they would be able to worship freely. Upon their request, the Messenger of Allah spoke to them and said, "Go to the land of the Abyssinians. Allah will grant you relief there and there you will be reunited."

Thus, in the fifth year of Prophethood, a group of fifteen Muslims, ten men and five women, left Mecca and emigrated to Abyssinia, the country of the Christian king, the Negus. Our Prophet's son in law, Uthman ibn Affan, and his daughter, Ruqayyah, were also a part of this group. The Qurayshi non-believers noticed them as they left Mecca and they ran after them. Yet, because the Muslims had long boarded the boat and put out to the Red Sea, the non-believers were not able to catch them.

The Abyssinian ruler, Negus, welcomed the Muslims and assisted them in every way possible. When the Qurayshi non-believers heard that the believers were doing well, they sent delegates to Abyssinia to ask Negus to turn the Muslims over to them. They did not want the believers to gain power. Negus, however, did not accept their requests and refused to hand over anyone that had taken refuge in his land.

Both Hamza and Umar

The Quraysh were not happy with Negus's response but they did not have the power to confront him and resist. Events that would surely take away their bliss was to come in the following days anyway. The thing that the non-believers feared the most was for the two most powerful men in Mecca, Hamza and Umar, may Allah be pleased with them, to become Muslim. Everyone would shy away in the presence of these men who radiated an air of rigor to their surroundings. They knew very well that things would get extremely difficult if they too were to change lanes.

One day, Hamza ibn Abdul Muttalib, was returning from a hunting session and was equipped with his bow and arrows. As he was walking towards the Ka'ba he ran across a maid on the road. Out of breath, she exclaimed, "Hamza! Hamza! Do you have any idea what Abu Jahl did to your nephew Muhammad just now? He confronted Muhammad in an intimidating manner and talked abusively to him, giving him such a hard time.

All of a sudden, Hamza ibn Abdul Muttalib was filled with rage. He loved his nephew so much. The fact that his nephew was tyrannized without even being guilty for anything was what made him furious the most. Without stopping to greet anyone he rushed to the Ka'ba at full speed. As soon as Abu Jahl saw him coming, he started regretting what he had done, but now it was too late. Hamza went straight to Abu Jahl. Then he raised his bow and hit Abu Jahl about the head, saying, "How dare you speak unpleasant words to Muhammad? I, too, am from his religion, I, too, say what he says. Come; confront me if you have that power."

Abu Jahl was bleeding from Hamza's blow. Hamza left him there as he was and went straight to his nephew, Muhammad, the Trustworthy. He gave the glad tidings that he would be at his side, always, from that point on, and said, "O Muhammad! I am certain you represent that which is true and virtuous. O my brother's son! Continue preaching your religion and conveying your message with no worry at all, any more! I swear to Allah that from this moment on, not even the brightness of the sun has more importance for me! For I have found my religion at last!"

Hamza's acceptance of the faith had become a great source of joy for the Muslims. Henceforth, the Qurayshi non-believers would have to take Hamza's being into account before deciding to attack the believers.

All of Mecca was talking about Hamza and his acceptance of the faith. Leaders of the Quraysh wanted to put an end to this dangerous spread of Islam once and for all. According to them, the only way to achieve this would be to kill Muhammad! Killing him would be a very risky task. For they knew that if they were to do such a thing, a never-ending blood feud between them and the sons of Abdul Muttalib could very well start. As they were speaking amongst themselves in Daru'n-Nadwa, Umar ibn al-Khattab al-Faruq, who was quietly listening to them close by, spoke out angrily, "I will take care of this." He put on his weapons and set out on his way.

He was infuriated. As he was hurrying down the road, he ran into Nuaym. A Companion that was keeping his Muslim identity a secret, Nuaym asked, "Umar!" What is this rush? Where are you going?"

"I am on my way to kill this man that has divided our people and disapproved of our gods," Umar replied.

Nuaym was flustered; he had to figure out a way to stall for time. He said to Umar, "If you do such a thing, do you really think that the sons of Abdul Muttalib will keep you alive? Besides, your sister Fatima and her husband Said are a part of them also. Take care of your own family first."

Umar's fury had risen to another level. If Nuaym was telling the truth, then, for sure, he had to kill his sister and brother-in-law first. He changed his course and doubled his speed towards his sister's home. Right when he approached their door, he heard a voice coming from the inside. When he paid careful attention to the voice, he realized that it was the Qur'an being read. The words of Allah had captivated him, just like they had a couple years before, but he quickly got himself together and started pounding on the door. Meanwhile, he was shouting out with his booming voice and demanding that they open the door at once.

The folks inside were startled as they heard Umar's voice calling at the door. Habbab was inside, teaching them the Qur'an. The first thing they did was hide him in a corner of the house. Then they hid the verses of the Qur'an that they held in their hands. Fatima's fearful disposition as she was late opening the door made Umar even more restless. He asked right away, "What was that voice I just heard?"

"What voice? There was no voice," they replied.

"I heard it! I also heard that you too have accepted Muhammad's religion," he roared. Unable to stop himself, Umar ibn al-Khattab hit his brother-in-law with a severe blow.

When his sister Fatima attempted to stop him, he hit her as well. Covered in blood from Umar's blow, valiantly confronted her big brother and said, "Yes, we have become Muslim! We have put our faith in Allah and His Messenger. Go ahead, do what you want to do."

There was a deep silence in the room. For a while, Umar just stood still looking at his sister whom he had wounded.

Despite the situation she was in, she took a noble stance and stood up for her faith. The strength she attained through her faith was incredible. The great big Umar was starting to soften up. "Give me the page which you were reading when I was at the door," he said to his sister. They were a bit surprised. Fatima replied with hesitation, "We fear that you might harm them."

"Don't worry. I will not do anything to harm the pages," said Umar reassuringly. Then, he washed himself as Fatima taught him, took the pages with the verses in his hand and started to read them. At that moment, Habbab came out of where he was hiding. Turning to Umar he said, "O Umar! I swear to Allah that I wish for you to be blessed with the prayer of the Messenger of Allah. It was only yesterday that I heard him pray, 'O my Lord! Please strengthen your religion with one of these two Umars: Umar ibn al-Khattab or Amr

Prophet Muhammad: The Seal of All Prophets

ibn Hisham! 'I swear to Allah that his prayer has been accepted, O Umar."

The majestic Umar was now bent over and on his knees. He then turned to Habbab, saying,

"O Habbab! Take me to Muhammad."

Then, they set out on the road towards Arqam's house. While Umar ibn al-Khattab was on his way towards them, the Archangel Gabriel gave our Prophet the glad tidings that he was coming to embrace the faith. A short while later, Umar arrived, came inside, kneeled down on his knees in front of our Prophet and became a Muslim. This made the Messenger of Allah so happy that together with the Companions they cried out, "Allahu Akbar! Allahu Akbar! "Not wanting to keep this change bottled up inside himself, Umar was craving to exclaim his belief to all of Mecca. He turned to our Prophet saying, "O Messenger of Allah! If the non-believers are able to worship their idols Lat and Uzza freely, then why should we have to worship our Allah in secret?"

Our Prophet was quite pleased with this offer. From that point onwards, they had reached the strength to be able to announce the call to Islam out loud. They went out altogether and walked towards the Ka'ba. Such a scene made the non-believers very anxious. Abu Jahl came running and asked, "What is it that you want to do Umar?"

Umar's answer was very clear, "Whoever gives the Muslims a hard time, I will chop off their heads! *Ashadu an la ilaha illallah wa ashadu anna Muhammadan abduhu wa Rasuluh!* (I bear witness that there is no deity but Allah, and I bear witness that Muhammad is His servant and Messenger!) Those who know me, know me well. Those who don't, let them know that I am Umar ibn al-Khattab! Those who wish to leave their wife as a widow and their children as orphans, let them come and confront me!"

Such a courageous confrontation had frightened the Qurayshi non-believers. That day, the Muslims prayed in congregation at the Ka'ba for the first time. In this way, all the Arabs coming in to visit the Ka'ba also had a chance to witness the worship of Prayer in the religion of Islam.

The Second Emigration to Abyssinia

After seeing that the group who had emigrated to Abyssinia was very well received by the king, Negus, our Prophet decided to send a second group of Muslims—who were exposed to the tyranny of the non-believers—to the Abyssinian land. Leading the group, which emigrated to Abyssinia in the seventh year of Prophethood, was Abu Talib's son Jafar.

This group of 104 believers was made up of 83 men and 21 women. When they arrived in the Abyssinian land, Negus took them under his guardianship. They were safe now. They were also able to carry out their worship freely. As soon as they heard of this news, the Qurayshi non-believers chose Abdullah and Amr from among themselves to go to the ruler Negus with precious gifts in order to persuade him to return the Muslims.

Amr presented Negus with the most precious offerings, saying, "O emperor! These people that have taken refuge in your land; they have abandoned their religion and brought about a whole new religion. Their leaders ask of you to hand these individuals over to them."

"I will not make any decision before I have spoken to them first. I cannot allow any harm to be done to those who have taken refuge in my land," Negus replied.

Then he summoned the Muslim emigrants to his side and asked them, "This religion in which you believe, what kind of religion is it?"

The leader of the group of believers, Jafar, answered as follows, "O wise king! We used to be a people of ignorance, worshipping idols, eating unblessed meat, committing evil acts; a society where the powerful oppressed the weak. We were like this up until Allah sent us a trustworthy Messenger from amongst ourselves. Muhammad, peace and blessings be upon him, is the best from among us, and the Almighty Allah sent him as a Prophet to us. He called us to a journey towards Allah. He taught us that we should believe in the Oneness of Allah, worship Him alone, and stop worshipping the idols instead. He ordered us to speak the truth, to be faithful to our promises, to respect our relationship with our relatives and the rights of our neighbors, to stay clear of evil acts and bloodshed. Now, we believe in the One Allah and associate no partners with Him whatsoever. Those which He has forbidden, we accept as *haram* (forbidden) and those which He has set free, we accept as *halal* (permissible). It is for this reason that our close ones have declared enmity towards us. They have tortured us in order for us to reject our new faith. That is why we felt the need to take refuge in your country. We are happy to be under your guardianship, and we believe that no injustice will be done towards us as long as we are by your side."

Impressed by this explanation, Negus asked them to read a portion of the revelation that our Prophet conveyed. Upon this request, Jafar started reading the verses which described the births of the Prophets John and Jesus, peace be upon them. As Jafar finished reading the Divine message, Negus and the other priests were unable to hold back their tears. These were the words that flowed from Negus's mouth, "I swear to Allah, these are two lights radiating from the same lamp. Both Prophet Moses and Prophet Jesus had informed us of the same truth." He then turned to the Qurayshi delegates and said, "You may leave now, there is no way that I will ever turn them over to you."

Amr had no intention to give up on the issue so easily. The next day he appeared in Negus's presence once more and declared, "They believe that Jesus is a mere servant. Did you know about this?"

Negus then summoned the Muslims to his side once more to ask them what they know of Prophet Jesus. "Tell me what you know about Jesus," he said to them.

Jafar replied, "The only thing we know about him is through what our Prophet has taught us. He is Allah's servant and Messenger. He is of Allah's spirit and His word that he has bestowed upon Mary (Maryam). "Jesus is nothing other than what you have said," was Negus's response.

His decision was final. Turning to the Muslim emigrants, he said, "You are safe in my country! Whoever attempts to oppress you will be punished! Even if gold, enough to cover mountains, are offered in return for you, I will not hand you over to anyone."

After that, he commanded that the gifts the Qurayshi non-believers had brought be returned to them immediately. Unable to achieve their goal, Amr and his friend had no other choice than to return to Mecca empty-handed. So certain that the Muslims would be returned, the Qurayshi were outraged when they learned what actually happened.

The Years of Boycott

Furious about their delegates returning with the loads of gifts they had sent to Abyssinia, the Qurayshi non-believers grew even more somber day by day, as they heard glad tidings of the Muslims in Abyssinia. Things had started to get completely out of their hands. The protection of the sons of Abdul Muttalib was so impossible to overcome that they were unable to harm the Messenger of Allah with a lasting effect. Whether they were Muslim or not, all of the Hashimites, except for Abu Lahab, were protecting Muhammad, the Trustworthy.

The non-believers knew they certainly had to find a permanent solution to this issue. Finally, one evening they gathered and came to a decision that was even worse than death. They declared a boycott and decided to cut all connections with the Muslims and those helping them. According to the boycott, they were to cut all ties with the sons of Hashim and Abdul Muttalib until the moment they handed the Prophet over to them. They were to be chased away from Mecca; no one would marry their sons or daughters, and they would be cut off from all their sources of food and water. In other words, they were deliberately going to be left to perish. When the people perished on their own in the harsh conditions of the desert, then there would be no blood feuds to

Prophet Muhammad: The Seal of All Prophets

worry about. They put down their decisions onto a written document and posted the covenant on the walls of the Ka'ba. Thus, in the beginning of the seventh year of Islam, the Messenger of Allah, the Muslims and the sons of Hashim who supported them, were all confined to the place they called the neighborhood of Abu Talib.

The intention of the Qurayshi non-believers was to discourage the believers through such behavior and, in the end, leave our Prophet with no support. However, the Muslims and the sons of Hashim, who were gathered under Abu Talib, were determined to endure every hardship and stand by our Prophet no matter what. One of our Prophet's uncles, Abu Lahab, on the other hand, was willing to condone even the deaths of his relatives and did not hesitate to unite with the non-believers.

This period, which lasted three years, was a tough time of great challenge and hardship for both the believers and their friends. Most of the time, they suffered from hunger and thirst. There were times when they were even desperate enough to eat tree leaves and pieces of skin. The cries of lamentation and hunger coming from the small children were impossible to bear. These acts of inhumanity did not trigger even the faintest feelings of regret or pity in the furious non-believers. They would even give the highest prices to the merchants in the caravans coming in to Mecca just to make sure they wouldn't buy anything from the Muslim caravans. Those who wished to secretly help out the believers punished in the severest ways.

During these years of boycott, the wealthy Muslims among them spent their entire fortunes trying to accommodate the needs of those in hardship. Once again, Allah's Messenger's biggest supporter was his loyal wife, Khadija, during these days of suffering. In addition to keeping our Prophet's spirits up at every single moment, she also put forward whatever she possessed to help the Muslims in need, with no hesitation at all. Khadija's devotion and selflessness continued on until she had spent every bit of what she had in this very cause. Such behavior on her part had formed a glorious example for those around her, and had also served as a means for other people's hearts to open up to Islam.

The Miracle of the Moon

It was the ninth year of Prophethood. The boycott towards the Muslims was still going on. Contrary to what the non-believers had hoped for, because of the hardships the Muslims had to endure, more people became aware of Islam and the religion spread out even more. Frustrated at not being able to stop the spread, some of the Qurayshi non-believers had a certain request from our Prophet. They said, "If you really are a Prophet, then split the Moon in half in this night with a full moon. Let it be so that one half is visible over Mount Abu Qubays and the other half over the Mount Quayqian."

In response to their request, the Messenger of Allah asked, "If I do as you ask, will you accept the faith?" "Yes! We will accept the faith," they answered.

Then, our Prophet prayed lengthily for a while to Allah the Almighty. After finishing his prayer, he raised his right hand and with his index finger drew a line right through the Moon. After this action, half of the moon was over Mount Abu Qubays while the other half was over the Mount Quayqian. Turning to the ones surrounding him, Allah's Messenger declared, "Let all of you be a witness!"

Nevertheless, even after witnessing such a miracle some of the non-believers merely said, "Muhammad put a spell over us."

Others said, "Even if Muhammad did put a spell over us, he couldn't have put it over others too! Let's ask the people who have come to Mecca from other places. Have they also seen what we have seen? If they have, then this means it's true. If they haven't then there's certainly magic in it."

When it was morning, they asked the people coming into Mecca. All of them affirmed that they too had seen the Moon split into two. Despite everything, the non-believers refused to believe even after witnessing this very obvious miracle.

The Boycott Ends

Within the three years that the boycott was standing many miracles such as the splitting of the Moon took place, and many who witnessed these miracles chose the way of Islam. Mansur had written down the text of the boycott document. His hands dried up after that. The last miracle to take place within this period was a woodworm eating up the boycott document which had been hanging on the wall inside the Ka'ba. The woodworm had left nothing of the document except the sentence that read, "Bismika Allahumma (I start with your Name O my Lord)." When Allah the Almighty informed our Prophet about the miracle he related it to his uncle, Abu Talib.

Abu Talib asked in surprise, "O my brother's son! Is that really so?" Our Prophet replied, "Yes, uncle! I swear to Allah that this is the truth."

Upon hearing this, Abu Talib went straight to the Ka'ba to talk to the non-believers.

"O people of Quraysh! My nephew tells me that a woodworm has eaten up the document which you have prepared. The only part left of it is the part in which Allah's Name is mentioned. Go on, bring the document to me! If my nephew has spoken the truth, we will never turn him over to you! And you will give up on this boycott once and for all! If what he tells me is not true, then I will turn him over to you," he said to them.

After hearing such definite statements from Abu Talib, they said, "Alright, we accept," and sent one from amongst them to bring over the document.

The situation was quite fascinating. Indeed, everything else besides Allah's Name had been eaten away by the wood-worm. The non-believers no longer had any words to say.

Gaining courage through this, Abu Talib scolded the others, saying, "I guess it's clear now who has been doing injustice, isn't that right?"

Not even one of them was able to answer Abu Talib. They condemned and blamed each other. "We've committed sheer tyranny towards our brothers," was all they could say, and they had no other choice than to lift the boycott. Three long years of trouble and suffering were finally over. The believers were grateful to their Lord for saving them from such grave hardships. There was an air of celebration throughout Mecca. Everyone had been reunited with their homes, spouses, friends and relatives.

After the boycott had been lifted, a group of Christians from Abyssinia came to Mecca. They had come to learn more about the religion of Islam, which they heard from the Muslims that had emigrated to their country. This Christian group met with our Prophet near the Ka'ba. They listened to the verses from the Qur'an with great respect. They were very much pleased with the answers our Prophet gave to every question that was directed to him. When the Messenger of Allah invited them to accept Islam as their faith, they all became Muslim and were crying tears of joy. They paid no attention to the non-believers who were watching them and in-sulting them as they accepted their new faith.

Their only response to them was, "We will not behave in the same ignorant way as you have towards us, and we will never turn back from this true religion that has been grant-ed to us."

The Year of Sorrow

Painful incidents were to follow the joy of being freed from the three-year period of life under boycott. Eight months after the boycott had been lifted, Abu Talib fell seriously ill. One day, a group of Qurayshi leaders came to visit him and said the following, "O Abu Talib! You know that we are proud of you. Nowadays, you have fallen very ill and we are afraid for you. The things that have been going on between us and your nephew are all obvious. Call him to your side and tell him to leave us at peace with our religion."

When Abu Talib summoned our Prophet to his side and told him of their offer, our Prophet said to the non-believers, "All right, let it be, but I want you to promise me one thing. This is a promise that will unite all Arabs and Persians under your rule."

Abu Jahl replied, "I swear upon your father that for this I would give not one but ten promises." When the Messenger of Allah said, "You must say, there is no deity but Allah, and you must give up on everything else you worship besides Him," in response, they clapped their hands in rejection and exclaimed, "O Muhammad! Are you going to turn all the gods into one single God?

Your suggestion is truly bizarre." Then, among themselves, they said, "This man is not going to give us anything we want. Let us go on our own path then and continue following the religion of our fathers until the day Allah makes His judgment between us."

After the others had left, Abu Talib said to our Prophet, "O my brother's son! As far as I can see, you did not ask for anything bad from them."

These words filled Allah's Messenger's heart with a longing for his uncle to become Muslim. He drew near and said to his uncle, "My uncle! Say those words so that I will be able to help you in the Day of Judgment." However, Abu Talib's response was, "O my brother's son! If I didn't fear that the Quraysh would think that I said those words because I was afraid of death, I would say them and I would make you happy."

Our Prophet became very sad. He did not want his beloved uncle to die before embracing faith. A few days later, Abu Talib's illness grew even worse. Our Prophet and his uncle, Abbas, were at Abu Talib's side. Just before Abu Talib closed his eyes and deceased, his brother Abbas noticed that his lips were moving and so, listened carefully. When he felt that he was uttering the words of the declaration of Allah's Oneness, he turned to our Prophet and said, "My brother Abu Talib was saying the words that you wanted him to say." Our Prophet, though, replied, "I did not hear him," as he was full of tears.

The Messenger of Allah was truly sorry that his uncle had died before accepting the faith. Abu Talib had loved our Prophet even more than he loved his own sons. He had protected our Prophet against the non-believers despite all odds. From now on, our Prophet was left without his greatest protection.

Following Abu Talib's decease, the Messenger of Allah was going to be shaken with another great sorrow. His loyal, faithful spouse, his companion for life, Khadija was very ill. Our Prophet's heart was full of indescribable sorrow. His blessed wife was lying down in her bed worn out and exhausted. Once the richest woman in Mecca, she was now bent over in pain and hunger. There was a deep distress hidden in her eyes. She was not worried about dying; on the contrary, she welcomed it as a way to becoming eternal. Her only concern was that she was going to be separated from Allah's Messenger, leaving him alone with the many difficulties of life. Nonetheless, this was Allah's will. They were both saddened as they thought of the other's condition.

Only three days after Abu Talib's decease, Khadija's illness grew even worse. The blessed mother of the believers closed her eyes on the night of Qadr (Power), on the month of Ramadan in the tenth year of Prophethood. After all, she had been the first of many things. She had been the first to believe in Allah and His Messenger, the first to make ablution together with Allah's Messenger, and the first to perform the Prayers behind him. Now, she became the first martyr from Allah's Messenger's household.

Our Prophet himself lead the Funeral Prayer for his blessed wife and also placed her into her grave at the cemetery of Al-Hajun with his own hands. He covered the top of the grave with soil. With tears in his eyes, he watched the black soil for a long while, the soil which now covered over his beloved wife. The death of our blessed mother Khadija deepened the sorrow of our Prophet and the Muslims. Because of all the sorrow they endured, one after the other, the Messenger of Allah called that year "the Year of Sadness."

After his blessed wife passed away, our Prophet started coming out of his house less frequent than before. During the times that he did come out, he would be relating the new teachings that the Archangel Gabriel had brought. Other times, he would be inviting the non-believers to the religion of Islam, by reading to them from the Qur'an. The non-believers, however, were still set on denying him. The fact that Abu Talib and Khadija were no longer around had given them much more courage. They started harming Allah's Messenger even more.

On the other side, the fact that Khadija was not with him anymore had really affected the Messenger of Allah. He was always thinking of their memories together. The Messenger of Allah was now both a mother and a father to his daughters, and with their mother's death they too were deeply saddened and sorrowful. Especially the youngest of our Prophet's daughters, Fatima, was frequently asking about her mother. The Messenger of Allah comforted his daughters by telling them that the Archangel Gabriel had brought greetings from their Lord to Khadija and had given the glad tidings of a house in Paradise, a house made of pearls. Khadija was a virtuous woman very much worthy of Allah's greetings and His Messenger's praise. She was a faithful and devout wife and a role model for mothers, in all aspects. The Messenger of Allah commended her by saying, "The most auspicious woman of the heavens is Mary, the daughter of Imran, and the most auspicious woman of the worlds is Khadija, the daughter of Khuwaylid." He always remembered his blessed wife. He spoke of her virtues for as long as he lived.

A Never-ending Enmity

Joyous over the recent deaths, the non-believers were ever more hostile towards the believers and our Prophet. Now that Abu Talib was out of the picture and they had complete control over the Quraysh they were much more comfortable to act as they pleased. They had previously accused the Messenger of Allah of being a magician. This time, they attacked him with even harsher insults. One day, as he was walking home, an unfortunate non-believer came after our Prophet and dumped soil over his blessed head. His young daughter, Fatima, saw our Prophet as he stepped inside. Seeing his father like this made her very sad. She rushed to fetch some water and started washing our Prophet's head. Tears quietly rolled down her cheeks as she washed her father. Our Prophet wiped away the tears in noble Fatima's eyes and said to his beloved child, "Don't cry my dear child. Allah will protect your father." He added, full of thought, "If it weren't for the death of my uncle Abu Talib, the non-believers would never have found the courage to insult me in such a way."

Days had passed and the season for pilgrimage had come again. Different tribes throughout Arabia were flocking into Mecca as they did every year. A festival of culture and entertainment had been set up near the Ka'ba. The Sultan of all Messengers was visiting the different tribes one by one, as he always did. People curious about this new religion followed him around and gathered wherever they saw him. On one of these days, the Messenger of Allah called out to the people in the festival grounds, and said to them, "O people! Say, 'La ilaha illallah (There is no deity but Allah)' and be saved." Hearing this, a man from amongst the crowd threw the stones in his hand towards our Prophet and cried, "O people! Beware of believing what he says, for he is a liar."

The stones that were thrown at him had made our Prophet's blessed ankles bleed. Nonetheless, he continued to patiently deliver the message of Allah the Almighty.

A foreigner named Tariq had witnessed this incident. He asked those who were standing there, "Who is this man?"

"He is from the sons of Abdul Muttalib," they replied.

"And who is this other man who threw stones at him," he continued. "That is his uncle Abu Lahab," was their response.

Both Abu Lahab—who continued with his enmity throughout his entire life—and the other non-believers considered it an achievement to insult the Messenger of Allah at every single opportunity. Another one of these opportunities was the day when our Prophet was praying near the Ka'ba. Some of the Quraysh were sitting near the place where our Prophet stood in the presence of his Almighty Lord. For an instant, they noticed that our Prophet spent quite some time in prostration. They wanted to take advantage of this opportunity to mock him.

One of the non-believers caught sight of a camel's tripe and conjured up an insidious plan.

"Which one of you will go fetch the camel's tripe and dump it on Muhammad's back when he goes down to prostration," he asked sleazily.

Uqba who was sitting among them said, "I'll do it," in an insolent manner, and stood up.

He grabbed the tripe, brought it over and dumped it on our Prophet's back. They all started rolling over with laughter. The Messenger of Allah, on the other hand, did not even bother to lift his head from prostration. A merciful and right-minded man who saw the incident from afar ran to Fatima, our Prophet's daughter, to inform her of what was going on. The situation made Fatima truly unhappy. She immediately ran over to her beloved father's side. She took a hold of the tripe and threw it over to the side. Our Prophet completed his prostration, raised his head, and turned towards the Ka'ba. He raised his hands and prayed out loud against the seven people who were present there. Their laughter died out upon hearing the negative words about themselves. They had grown fearful of the prayer that our Prophet had made against them. They too knew very well that the prayers made in the Ka'ba would for sure be answered.

The Days of Ta'if

The insults and defamation from the non-believers was constantly increasing. The Messenger of Allah decided to step out of Mecca to keep away from the unpleasant environment for a while. He also wished to be able to perform his duty in other places. He took his adopted child Zayd with him and they travelled to Ta'if together. They stayed here for about ten days. Allah's Messenger called the idol-worshipping people there to believe in the Existence and Oneness of Allah the Almighty. Unfortunately, after all the meetings and encounters during his stay in Ta'if there was not even a single person willing to believe and help him. Afraid that their youth would become Muslim, the people of Ta'if did not accept our Prophet's offer. They asked him, "Could Allah not find another man besides you to send as Prophet?" "You may go wherever you like so long as you leave our land," they told him.

Then they ridiculed and mocked our Prophet. As if that were not enough, they gathered a dissolute group from the people and placed them on the two sides of the road through which our Prophet would pass. These immoral persons injured the Messenger of Allah by attacking him with stones as he passed through them. All the while, Zayd was selflessly trying to protect our Prophet. He used his body as a shield to guard against the stones that were being thrown. Despite all their effort, the Messenger of Allah was injured and his blessed feet were covered in blood. Zayd's head had also been hit by the stones. Through extreme hardship, they were finally able to take refuge in Utba and Shayba's vineyard. The Messenger of Allah first tended to Zayd's wound before taking care of his own. After sitting down for a bit and resting in the shade of a hanging grape vine he performed a two-unit Prayer, raised his hands and prayed to Allah the Almighty, "Everything is for Your sake alone and all power and strength is in Your hands!"

Meanwhile, a distant relative of our Prophet who owned the gardens had sent them grapes with his slave Addas. Our Prophet uttered the words "In the Name of Allah" before starting to eat the grapes. The slave Addas, who was a Christian, was taken aback upon these words that he heard. "I have never heard such words before. What kind of words are these?" he exclaimed.

Our Prophet smiled at Addas and asked him where he was from. "I am from the people of Nineveh," he replied. Upon his response the Messenger of Allah declared, "The land of my brother Yunus."

Full of curiosity, Addas asked our Prophet how he knew about Yunus, peace be upon him. The fulfilling responses he received from Allah's Messenger and the tidings of a last Prophet which he had previously heard from the priests were enough for Addas to embrace this new faith.

A short while later, our Prophet and Zayd got up to leave this dangerous place. Our Prophet's tender heart had been seriously hurt and his mind was preoccupied as they slowly headed towards Mecca. It was only until they reached a place called Salib that he was able to recover and come to himself. When he raised his head, he noticed that there was a cloud shading over him. A short while later, he saw the Archangel Gabriel also. Gabriel called to our Prophet, "Allah the Almighty is aware of all that your people have said to you. He has sent the Archangel of the mountains to you. Whatever outcome you wish for your people, the Archangel will be at your command."

Meanwhile, the Archangel of the mountains greeted our Prophet. Pointing to the mountains surrounding Mecca, the Archangel said, "O Muhammad! I am the Archangel of the mountains! Your wish is my command. If you wish so, I will close these two mountains over Ta'if at once."

Allah's Messenger's response beautifully portrayed the degree of his mercy and compassion even towards the ones who denied and insulted him.

"No indeed! I do not wish for them to be destroyed. I only wish that Allah will bring about righteous ones from among them in the generations to come, righteous individuals that will worship only Allah and not associate any partners with Him."

Our Prophet and Zayd then continued on their way. After performing the Morning Prayer in a place near Mecca called Nahla, they finally reached Mecca.

The Ascension

E leven years had passed since the coming of the first revelation in the cave of Hira. Despite all the efforts and en-
deavors of the Messenger of Allah, the Meccan non-believers
had been persistent in their denial and had increased their insults and oppression with each passing day. The way the Meccans had started to treat him after the deaths of Abu Talib and
Khadija, the things they encountered in Ta'if and the way the
people ridiculed them when they returned to Mecca, all of
these had especially weighed our Prophet down.

One evening, as the Messenger of Allah was sitting in the
Ka'ba, the Archangel Gabriel appeared right beside him. This
coming was very different from the previous ones. With him
there was a riding animal that was a little bigger than a donkey but a little smaller than a mule; it was named Buraq. Archangel Gabriel opened up our Prophet's bosom and washed it
clean with Zamzam water. Then he poured a golden bowl
filled with belief and wisdom into our Prophet's open bosom
and closed it back up.

Afterwards, they embarked on an indescribable journey
together with the noble Prophet. The Buraq, which our beloved Prophet was riding on, moved so fast that every step he
took was to the last visible point in the horizon. They travelled
at the speed of lightning. They arrived at the Al-Aqsa Mosque

in no more than an instant. Allah's Messenger dismounted the Buraq and headed towards the mosque to perform his Prayer. Meanwhile, Archangel Gabriel tied the Buraq to a column that stood there. Prophet Abraham and Prophet Moses, peace be upon them, were also among the group of Prophets, who were awaiting our Prophet's arrival. They stood in congregation and the Messenger of Allah lead them in Prayer. After that the Archangel of revelation invited him to a journey far beyond the heaves and skies. They rose through the different levels of the skies and as they ascended they were met with a different ceremony at each level. At each gate of the heavens they met with a different Prophet. Each one prayed for them and congratulated them.

During this mysterious journey of Ascension, Allah's Messenger had also seen the gardens of Paradise and the pits of Hell. They ascended even more. When they reached a point called Sidrat'ul-Muntaha, the Archangel Gabriel said, "If I were to take even one step further down this road, I would burn up." And so, our Prophet continued his journey alone.

He continued on to places that no one besides Allah the Almighty knew or had seen. A matchless beauty covered over everything. It was a beauty impossible to describe with the expressions within our knowledge. And, the Messenger of Allah met with Allah the Almighty without any barrier in between. The Daily Prayers were rendered obligatory during this Divine meeting. From then on, the ascension of every believer would be through the performing of Daily Prayers.

The time for their return drew near, and our Prophet found himself back in Mecca. The first people to hear of this miraculous journey were those closest to our Prophet. Afterwards, he came out of his home to tell the people of Mecca the things that he had experienced. The Messenger of Allah went to the Ka'ba and started telling people of his Miraj, holy journey of Ascension. Everyone was astonished as they heard the things which the Messenger of Allah narrated. The things he spoke of were things that were impossible for an individual to achieve by themselves. The All Powerful Allah had shown His Divine power to the people by taking His most beloved servant on such a journey.

The crowd that stood before him asked our Prophet many questions about that specific night. They searched for proof and special signs embedded in his answers. They even asked him to describe the Mosque in Al-Aqsa. Of all the questions that the Meccans asked our Prophet, not even a single one was left unanswered. Just then, Abu Jahl happened to be passing by the Ka'ba. When he noticed the crowd and learned what was going on, he slyly caressed his beard. He had found himself a new way of ridicule. He turned to our Prophet and said,

"If I gather your people here, will you explain this exact situation to them as well?"

When the Messenger of Allah replied, "Yes," Abu Jahl started calling out at the top of his lungs.

Now, there was no one left in Mecca who had not heard of the Ascension of Allah's Messenger. The non-believers rushed over to Abu Bakr to inform him of the situation. They thought to themselves, "He will not believe in what has happened anyway and will stop following Muhammad's way from now on. "However, Abu Bakr's attitude came as a big disappointment for them. His answer was short and crystal clear; "If the Messenger of Allah claims that this is so, then it must be the truth!"

After such a display of submission, the Messenger of Allah gave his faithful friend the name As-Siddiq, the Eminently Truthful person.

The Allegiances of Aqaba

It was the eleventh year of Islam, and this year too, like all other years, Mecca was filled with Arabs coming from afar and near during the season of pilgrimage. As always, Allah's Messenger had gone out to see the visitors coming into Mecca and to call them to have faith. On one of these days, somewhere in between Mecca and Mina, on a hill called Aqaba, he came across six people who were coming from Medina. He recited the Qur'an for them and called them to Islam. These six people were from the Khazraj tribe in Medina. After listening to our Prophet, they accepted Islam right away. Thus, they became the first people from Medina to embrace Islam. They agreed to meet the Messenger of Allah again, at the same place when they came back for the next hajj, or pilgrimage, season and left for Medina. Back home, they started to explain Islam to their people. A year later, during the next hajj season, six more people came along with the previous six, and they met with the Messenger of Allah. These twelve people from Medina pledged their allegiance to our Prophet by saying,

"We will obey you at all times, including times that are both peaceful and troublesome, both joyful and sorrowful! We will always prefer you over ourselves. We will not object to orders, no matter who the authority may be. We will not be intimidated by those who ridicule us in the path of Allah. We will not associate partners of any kind with Allah. We will not steal and will not come near adultery. We will never attempt to kill our children. We will never defame or slander each other. We will never go against you in any good that you do."

Then they said, "O, Messenger of Allah! The non-believers will gather at Mina tomorrow. Give us permission to slay them all with our swords." Our Prophet declared, "This is certainly not what Allah has ordered. If you stay true to your oaths, then your reward will be in the gardens of Paradise. But, if you break your oath for whatever reason, Allah is the only One who will either punish or forgive you."

This meeting would later be called the Allegiance of Aqaba. The people of Medina asked our Prophet to send them a teacher who would teach them about Islam and how to read the Qur'an. That was right about the time that Mus'ab ibn Umayr had returned from Abyssinia. The Messenger of Allah chose Mus'ab to be their teacher. He sent Mus'ab to Medina together with the believers who had pledged their allegiance to our Prophet at Aqaba. And so, Mus'ab became the first Companion of our Prophet to emigrate to Medina. There, he would represent the Messenger of Allah. He would be the one to teach the people this new religion that they had just been introduced to. Only a year later, in the thirteenth year of Islam, during the season of pilgrimage, Mus'ab came back to Mecca with seventy-two believers following him. He spoke to our Prophet and gave him the glad tidings that Islam was spreading ever so fast in Medina. He said, "O Messenger of Allah! There is no household left in Medina into which Islam has not entered and is not being spoken of."

Our Prophet and his Companions were overjoyed with this news. This third meeting between the believers from Medina and our Prophet was to be called the second Allegiance of Aqaba.

Our Prophet had come to the meeting with his uncle Abbas, who had not yet believed in Islam. During this meeting they talked about the details of the emigration to Medina. The believers promised that they would always obey Allah and His Messenger no matter what; that they would protect our Prophet from all enemies; that they would never hesitate in doing the right thing; and that they would sacrifice their lives and their belongings in this cause.

After this pledge of their allegiance, our Prophet chose twelve representatives from among those coming from Medina and appointed them as head of their tribes. It was only until after everything was complete that the non-believers became aware of what was going on because the believers had been very clever in coming to the meeting separately and in secret. As a result, they had been powerless in preventing the positive developments.

Farewell to Mecca

Thanks to the last Aqaba allegiance, Medina had become a safe haven for the Muslims. As a result of the tyranny and oppression of the non-believers, the Muslims were no longer able to sustain living in Mecca. Upon this, Allah the Almighty granted the believers permission to emigrate to the city of Medina. Thus, in the fourteenth year of the Prophethood, the Muslims began leaving Mecca in small groups. As a result of the oppression and tyranny they had been exposed to on their path to Allah, they were once again abandoning their close ones and their belongings and emigrating for the very sake of Allah.

The decision for this emigration had been finalized in the month of Dhu al-Hijjah, during the last meeting at Aqaba for allegiance with the Muslims from Medina. And, the permission for the emigration had been granted in the beginning of the month of Muharram. The Qurayshi non-believers wanted to be rid of their enemies, on one hand, but were a bit concerned about their departure, on the other. Most of the believers emigrated in secret so as to be safe from the harm of the non-believers. Umar ibn al-Khattab, though, girded on his sword, took his arrows and spear with him, and after circumambulating the Ka'ba, openly challenged the enemies of Islam. Afterwards, he started the journey towards

Medina in broad daylight, taking twenty other believers with him. On account of their fear of Umar, not one person was able to interfere with this group. As time went on, the believers that were left behind continued to emigrate to Medina in small groups. This changing of place that the Muslims went through for the sake of their religion was called the Emigration, or Hijra; they were called the Muhajir, and their hosts living in Medina who opened up their houses for them were called the Ansar.

The Messenger of Allah had sent nearly all of the believers to Medina safe and sound. The ones left behind were Abu Bakr, Ali ibn Abu Talib, and a few members of our Prophet's family. The Qurayshi non-believers knew that our Prophet was going to emigrate to Medina as well. If he reached Medina, this could mean disaster for them in the future. Locking him up in prison was not a very reliable solution. As the non-believers thought over and over on how they could stop our Prophet, in the end, they came to the conclusion that they needed to kill him. Satan himself, disguised as a hideous old man, was also at the meeting where they came to this decision. They found a simple yet effective solution in order to prevent a possible blood feud among our Prophet's tribe. The duty was assigned to a certain gang chosen from among the different tribes within the city. This way, they couldn't blame just one person, and our Prophet's tribe wouldn't have the courage to stand up to all the tribes in the city at the same time. The idea came from Abu Jahl and even Satan liked the idea very much.

While the non-believers continued on with their preparations to kill our Prophet, Allah the Almighty sent His Messenger the command to emigrate. The Archangel Gabriel also came to tell him of the non-believers' plans, and told him not to sleep in his bed that night. And so, our Prophet told Abu Bakr that they were finally going to leave the city. For months Abu Bakr had been waiting for this news. He had even bought two camels for this. They agreed to meet each other that night. Abu Bakr gathered some food and drinks for the journey and also arranged for someone to guide them along the path.

Though the people of Mecca refused to believe in the religion that Allah's Messenger had brought, due to his infallible trustworthiness they still trusted him with their valuables and precious belongings and put them in his custody. Our Prophet took utmost care of the things that were entrusted to him, and so, he wanted to return all the valuables to their rightful owners, even those who wanted to kill him, before emigrating. Ali was going to lie in our Prophet's bed that night. He was to return the valuables to their owners in the morning and then he too would emigrate to Medina after them.

On the night that Allah's Messenger was to emigrate, Ali fell asleep in our Prophet's bed. The assassins surrounded our Prophet's home and started waiting for him to step outside. Our Prophet opened the door and stepped outside to where the non-believers were on the lookout for him. He picked up a handful of earth and threw it at the assassins while he recited the first nine verses of Surah Yasin. Allah the Almighty kept them occupied with the dirt in their eyes, and miraculously, they were unable to notice our Prophet standing there. He merely walked away from amongst them. At the same time, Abu Bakr was also under surveillance. He looked out the window of his home and secretly sneaked out to meet with the Messenger of Allah. They climbed towards the summit of the Mount Light in the pitch darkness of the night.

After a while, a man approached the ones who were waiting in front of our Prophet's door, and asked them, "What are you waiting for here?" "We are waiting for Muhammad," they answered.

The man said, "Muhammad is long gone. See, he even threw some dirt on your heads before leaving." Outraged over what they heard, they yelled, "We swear we did not see him coming out."

They barged into the Messenger's home. Excited to see that someone was sleeping in his bed, "Now there's Muhammad! He's asleep in his bed," they cried.

When they lifted the covering and realized that it was Ali that was lying in bed, they froze in disbelief. They were infuriated.

"Where is Muhammad?" they asked him angrily.

"I do not know," replied Ali.

They left him just like that and hurried out of the house in search of our Prophet's trail. Meanwhile, the Messenger of Allah had long reached his faithful Companion Abu Bakr's house and they had started walking towards the Mount Light. As they were climbing up the mountain, Abu Bakr walked in front of our Prophet for some time and then changed position to walk behind him. When the Messenger of Allah noticed that he was constantly doing this, he asked Abu Bakr why he was doing so. Abu Bakr answered, "O Messenger of Allah! When I remember that the non-believers are searching for you I start walking behind you, when I remember that they are on the lookout for you I start walking in front of you."

When our Prophet asked, "Would you prefer a disaster meant for me to strike you instead," Abu Bakr replied, "Definitely! I swear to Allah, who sent you with the true religion, that I would prefer a disaster to strike me rather than strike you."

After an hour of walking, they finally arrived at the cave on the Mount Light. As they reached the entrance of the cave, Abu Bakr called out to our Prophet, "O Messenger of Allah! Let me enter first."

He cleaned the inside of the cave and checked over everything very carefully. He covered all the holes with pieces of cloth that he tore from his shirt so as to prevent a snake or a scorpion coming out and harming Allah's Messenger. Then, he turned to our Prophet and said, "You may enter now o Messenger of Allah."

Our Prophet went inside the cave. He was so exhausted that he fell asleep as soon as he put his blessed head down on Abu Bakr's lap. Meanwhile, Abu Bakr realized that one of the holes in the ground was left open. He had run out of the cloth that he used to close up the holes. So, he used his foot heel to close up the hole so that no snake could come out and harm our Prophet. A short while later, a snake rose out of that hole and bit Abu Bakr's foot. Despite the pain he felt on his heel, Abu Bakr did not even move a muscle so as not to disturb our Prophet. The pain, however, caused tears to fall from his eyes. When the tears dropped onto our Prophet's face, he woke up immediately. When he realized what had happened, he wet his had with his blessed saliva and spread it over the snake bite. The pain on Abu Bakr's heel was gone in an instant. His foot was healed in no time; it was like the snake had never bit him.

Meanwhile, the Meccan non-believers were looking everywhere for the Messenger of Allah and Abu Bakr. What's more, they had even announced a big reward of money to whoever found them. Every person old enough to carry a sword in Mecca had started out in search of them. After searching high and low, all over Mecca for our Prophet and his faithful Companion with no success, they searched all of the mountains surrounding Mecca. Then they gathered those who were renowned for their courage and sent them off on their horses, outside of Mecca, to follow their trail.

As the Meccan non-believers continued on their search, with a single command from Allah the Almighty, a tree grew right in front of their cave, a tree big enough to cover our Prophet's face and hide their position. Along came a spider and weaved its web in between the tree and the cave. Two mountain pigeons came and nested right between the spider and the tree.

Meanwhile, the non-believers who were following their trail had reached the cave in the Mount Light. The tracer who was guiding them turned to the ones standing beside him and said, "There is a trace on that rock right there. Where they went after that, I do not know. I swear to Allah that the people you are looking for have not gone beyond this cave."

Turning to their guide, the non-believers said, "To this day, we have never seen you falter." A few men girded with swords approached the cave and one of them went up to the entrance to look inside. However, they all stood in amazement and confusion when they saw the pigeon nest and the spider web because that was exactly where the footsteps came to an end. They turned to each other saying, "If they had entered the cave, there wouldn't be a spider web in the doorway. If there were people inside the cave, the pigeons would not have nested right here."

When a few of them suggested, "Let's go inside and take a look," Umayya ibn Khalaf objected.

"Have you no minds? What are you going to do in the cave? Are you really going to enter this cave that has layers of spider webs in its entrance? I swear to Allah, if you ask me, this spider web was weaved before Muhammad was even born," he said.

The non-believers were so close that if they were to kneel down and look inside they could very well see both our Prophet and Abu Bakr. Abu Bakr became deeply worried that his dear friend would be harmed. With a trembling voice he whispered, "If they kill me, I am only one person. I will die and be off. But if they kill you, then the entire community will perish!"

Our Prophet was standing in Prayer while Abu Bakr was keeping a lookout. As our Prophet finished his Prayer, Abu Bakr turned to him saying, "Your tribe is still searching for you! I swear to Allah that I am not worried for myself. But I fear that something undesirable will happen to you."

Seeing Abu Bakr's concern, our Prophet turned to him and spoke in a very calm manner. "O Abu Bakr! Have no fear! Surely, Allah is with us and is protecting us," he said reassuringly.

Looking at the feet of the non-believers just above their heads right outside the cave entrance, Abu Bakr said, "O

Prophet of Allah! If any one of them were to look down, they would certainly be able to see us." Our Prophet replied, "O Abu Bakr! We are only two men, yet Allah is the third one among us." Abu Bakr said, "O Messenger of Allah! If one of them were to raise their foot and look down, they would see us right underneath their feet."

And our Prophet replied, "Don't be upset, Allah is with us! O Abu Bakr! Don't underestimate two men when Allah is the third one among them."

When they realized that our Prophet and Abu Bakr weren't there either, not wanting to waste any more time, the non-believers went back to Mecca in disappointment. Back in Mecca, they announced high and low that they would give a total of one hundred camels to whoever found and brought our Prophet and Abu Bakr to them, dead or alive.

Our Prophet and Abu Bakr stayed in the cave for three days. During the daytime, Abu Bakr's son Abdullah walked around in the streets among the Qurayshi, listening to what they spoke about Abu Bakr and the Messenger of Allah and learning their plans of conspiracy. At night, he would go to the cave to inform them of what was happening. Amir ibn Fuhaira, a freedman that used to be Abu Bakr's slave, would graze Abu Bakr's sheep together with the other Meccan shepherds during the daytime. When it was nighttime, he would bring the sheep over to the cave. There they would milk the sheep and slaughter one for food. When morning came, Abdullah would leave the cave, and Amir would follow after him with his herd, thus covering up Abdullah's tracks.

Abdullah ibn Urayqit was going to guide them on their journey to Medina. On the night of their third day, he came to the cave, just as they had agreed. Our Prophet, Abu Bakr, Abu Bakr's former slave Amir ibn Fuhaira and Abdullah ibn Urayqit, who would be their guide, all set out on the road towards Medina. After covering some distance, the Messenger of Allah stopped in his tracks and turned around to look back at Mecca once more. He was deeply saddened by the fact that he was leaving his home country where he was born and raised, that he was being separated from this holy land in which the Ka'ba stood. Abu Bakr shared these same feelings. After pausing for a moment, the Messenger of Allah called out,

"I swear to Allah, O Mecca! I know, without a doubt, that you are the best of all the places that Allah has created and you are the most beloved place in the eyes of Allah! If your people had not forced me out, I would never have left you."

These words from the Messenger of Allah made Abu Bakr very emotional. He uttered the words, "Inna lillahi wa inna ilaihi raji'un" (Surely, we belong to Allah and to Him we are bound to return). They drew the Messenger of Allah from his home! Surely, they too will perish one day," and they continued on their way.

They were completely out of Mecca now. The blessed group travelled night and day towards the city of Medina. Meanwhile, the Qurayshi non-believers had no intention of giving up on their pursuit. They were still searching for them everywhere, trying to pick up on their trail. They had announced and spread the news that they were going to award whoever found our Prophet and Abu Bakr with one hundred camels for each.

The news had spread all the way to the land of the sons of Mudlij. This land also happened to be located on the route that the blessed group was travelling through. A few people from the sons of Mudlij were sitting together in a group when they heard of this award. Known throughout the land for his valor and courage, Suraqa ibn Ju'shum was also among the group. A man from the sons of Mudlij came to them as they were sitting together, turned to Suraqa and said to him,

"O Suraqa! I saw shadows of a couple of travelers walking towards the direction of the coast as they passed in front of me a little further in the distance. I think they may have been Muhammad and Abu Bakr."

Suraqa understood right away that their tracks had been found. He was overjoyed yet he didn't want the others around him to notice. He wanted to keep the award from the Quraysh to himself. He signaled for the man to be quiet, so as not to alert the others, and he said, "Those travelers that you saw were not Muhammad and his friend. You must have seen this and this man! They must have gone by here just now as well."

"You may be right," the man replied.

Later on, Suraqa girded himself with his sword and suit of armor and set off on our Prophet and Abu Bakr's trail. He rode his horse to a full gallop so that he could reach them as soon as possible. Before long, he spotted their tracks. He had come so close that he could even hear their voices now. Abu Bakr noticed that he was coming behind them. He turned to our Prophet, full of fear and panic and said, "O Messenger of Allah! This man is searching for us! We have been caught." Our Prophet, though, calmly turned toward him, and said, "Do not fear! Allah is with us."

Again, Abu Bakr said, "O Messenger of Allah! This man was searching for us and now he has found us," and tears welled up in his eyes. When our Prophet asked Abu Bakr why he was crying, his reply was, "I swear to Allah I am not crying for myself! I am crying for you."

Our Prophet turned around, looked at Suraqa and started praying. "O our Lord! Help us overcome this man in whichever way You please! Drive away any harm that will come from him! Make him fall off of his horse," he prayed.

Our Prophet's prayers were answered at that very moment. The horse stumbled over something and fell over onto the ground. Suraqa fell off his horse and rolled over onto the ground as well, but he picked himself up right away, got back on his horse and continued riding after them. Suraqa had gotten so close that he could even hear the prayer that the Messenger of Allah was speaking. Then, all of a sudden, the front two legs of Suraqa's horse sunk up to the knees into the sand. The horse was struggling to get back up yet it couldn't manage in any way to get its feet out of the sand. Suraqa had finally understood that our Prophet and his beloved Companion were being protected by Allah Himself. Helpless, he turned to them and cried out, "Help!"

"I am Suraqa ibn Ju'shum! Look at me! I want to talk to you. I swear to Allah that I will not cause any harm to you anymore. Nothing unpleasant will come to you from my hands! O Muhammad! I understand now that all that has happened to me is tied to your prayers! Pray to Allah for me so that He may save me from this situation I have fallen into! Let it be a debt upon my head; I swear to Allah that I will not tell the ones who are coming after me of your situation! Here is my pouch of arrows! Take one of these arrows! Come by my camels and goat and take whatever you need."

Our Prophet cried out in response, "I do not need any of your camels or goat." He prayed to Allah once again. The horse that had just been buried into the sand, shook off the sand, and got up on its feet just like that.

"Your tribe has promised an award of one hundred camels to whoever either kills you or brings you in captivity," said Suraqa as he told them of everything that the Quraysh were planning to do to our Prophet and Abu Bakr. He wanted to help them by giving them whatever they needed, but they refused to accept anything.

Suraqa then asked out Prophet to write him a note of sanctuary that would serve as a kind of omen between each other. Turning to Abu Bakr, our Prophet said, "Write a note for him."

Abu Bakr wrote the note that he was asked to write, on a small piece of leather, and gave the note to Suraqa. Suraqa took the note and put it inside his arrow pouch.

"O Messenger of Allah! Whatever you wish from me is my command," he nobly stated. In response, our Prophet said, "Stay right here! Do not let the others that are following us proceed from here." Suraqa stayed and made whoever he encountered along the way turn back, saying to them, "I am more than enough to tackle them here on your behalf."

The Most Beautiful Day

The blessed group had continued on with their journey and had finally reached the village of Quba, a little south of Medina. The Messenger of Allah decided to stay in the village of Quba for a couple of days with his group. They built a small mosque there right away. The Messenger of Allah and the believers accompanying him took off towards Medina the following Friday. As they were passing through the valley of Ranuna they realized that it was time for the Noon Prayer. They stopped for a while; the Messenger of Allah delivered a sermon and led the believers in the very first congregational Friday Prayer. After the Prayer, they started once again towards Medina.

The people of Medina had long heard of the news that our Prophet had started his journey. Everyone was full of excitement, waiting the moment of his arrival. Every day, they would gather atop a hill overlooking the surroundings, waiting for the travelers to arrive. At the end of the day, seeing that no one was arriving yet, they would go off in their separate ways. It was on one of these days that the people of Medina finally rejoiced with the unity they had all been yearning for. Every one of them rushed to Thaniyyati'l-Wada, or the valley of Al-Wada, as soon as they heard that the blessed group had arrived, our blessed Prophet had finally honored the city with his arrival.

The joy of the believers was at its peak as he entered their city. The blessed Messenger of Allah had risen over the people of Medina just like the moon rising over the black night. Women, men, children, servants, everyone was out in the streets rejoicing. This was truly to be their grandest festival. The believers were crying tears of joy and were reciting poetry. "O the white moon rose over us from the Valley of Wada! And we owe it to show gratefulness, where the call is to Allah! O Messenger, chosen from amongst us! You have surely come with the word to be obeyed." These were the verses rising over the skies of Medina. The Muslims in Medina had never rejoiced over anything as much as they rejoiced over the arrival of Allah's Messenger. Everyone called out, "Come to our home, O Messenger of Allah," and invited him to stay at their home. As they tried to take a hold of his camel's rein and direct it towards their own home, our Prophet said to them, "Let go of the camel's rein for the camel too has its own duty. It will go in whichever direction Allah commands him to go."

Our Prophet's camel was named Qaswa. Qaswa started walking. It reached a field that belonged to two orphans, Sahl and Suhayl, and knelt down in the field. A short while later, though, it got back on its feet and continued to walk. Qaswa knelt down once again, this time right beside the home of Abu Ayyub al-Ansari from the tribe of the Banu Najjar. At last, it was decided where our Prophet would be staying. Our Prophet stayed in that home for seven months.

Prophet Muhammad: The Seal of All Prophets

The Ansar and the Muhajirun
(The Helpers and the Migrants)

It had been five months since our Prophet had arrived in Medina. The Messenger of Allah organized a meeting in which the leaders of all the families from Mecca and Medina came together. In this meeting, he encouraged the Ansar to accept a sincere agreement in order to make life easier for the Muhajirun, who had left their homes behind for the sake of their religion. According to the agreement, an Ansari family from Medina, with suitable means, would open their home to a Muhajir family from Mecca. They would in this way be fully supportive of each other in complete brotherhood. Everyone agreed to this, and the Messenger of Allah appointed a certain number of the Muhajirun to the same number of Ansar. He also chose some of the believers from Mecca, separated them into pairs and declared them siblings, both amongst each other and also together with the believers from Medina.

This brotherhood was based on the principle of helping each other out, both materially and spiritually. The Messenger of Allah sought to increase the bond between the Meccans and Medinans, and the strength of Islam as a result. The Muslims of Medina were already racing against each other to host the Muhajir in their homes any way. In fact, there were even some who suggested, "O Messenger of Allah! Divide our gardens between our Muhajir brothers and ourselves as well! "Upon their request, the Messenger of Allah replied, "Act together in your daily efforts and workload, then share the fruits of your labor among yourselves afterwards."

This meant that from then on, everyone would work hard on doing their best and making great effort. In the end, the Meccan Muhajirun and the Medinan Ansar would share their harvest and live as one.

Emigrating to Medina had certainly been a breath of fresh air for the Muslims. They were setting up a new life for themselves by gathering around Allah's Messenger and the principals of the Islamic faith. The days of hardship and terror were long behind. In Medina, they were finally able to experience the serenity of worshipping in freedom and security.

When the Muslims of Medina brought our Prophet the very first fruit harvest of the year, he opened his hands and prayed; "O my Lord! Surely, Abraham was Your servant, friend and Prophet. I, too, am Your servant and Prophet! He had prayed to You for Mecca. And now, I pray to You for Medina. Whatever he wished for Mecca I wish for Medina, with twice the amount, from You."

He took the very first fruit of the year and, beckoning to the youngest child there, he handed the fruit to the child. With the blessing of our Prophet's prayer, Medina had become a city full of bliss for the people living there.

Al-Masjid an-Nabawi
(The Prophet's Mosque)

B ecause there was no *masjid*, or mosque, in Medina, in the beginning, congregational Prayer was performed in whichever place our Prophet happened to be. Now, there was a need for a *masjid*, a place in which the believers would gather, share verses from the Qur'an, perform Prayers, listen to the Messenger of Allah and find solutions to daily issues. There was a piece of land in which our Prophet's camel, Qaswa, had stopped and kneeled down, the very first day that the Messenger of Allah had entered Medina. After a short period of time, this piece of land was bought from their owners, and a masjid was built there. Our most beloved Prophet himself worked hard in the construction of the masjid, being the best example for the Muslims. One of his Companions saw him carrying the adobe bricks and said, "Give them to me, let me carry them for you."

"You are no more in need of Allah's mercy than I am," had been his reply. Rooms for the Messenger of Allah and his family had been constructed right next to the masjid. A new pulpit was constructed a short while after the construction of the masjid had been completed. Before that, our Prophet had been delivering his sermons whilst resting his arms on the stump of a date tree. The new pulpit was now standing over this tree stump. One day, while our Prophet was delivering his sermon, the tree stump starting sobbing and making noises like that of the bellow of a camel. All those present in the masjid had clearly heard this sound. Our Prophet asked the dried-up stump why it was crying and the stump answered that it was because of its separation from the Messenger of Allah. Our Prophet silenced its sobs, consoling it and giving it the glad tidings that it would continue its life in Paradise. When the stump had quieted down, the Prophet of compassion turned to his Companions and said, "If I had not shown love for the stump and consoled it so, it would have continued to cry like this until the Day of Judgment." Then, with our Prophet's orders, this date tree stump was buried underneath the newly-made pulpit.

From then on, the five Daily Prayers were performed in congregation inside this newly-constructed *masjid*. The Messenger of Allah was this *masjid*'s first and continuous leader in Prayer, orator and preacher. The duty of calling the believers to Prayer was given to Bilal al-Habashi from the very first day. Before, the Muslims would gather in front of the masjid at the Prayer times, which they would appoint according to the position of the sun. Because they estimated the Prayer times, the congregational Prayers weren't completely in order. Until then, the Muslims used to call one another to the Prayer with the words "As-salah, as-salah!" (Come to the Prayer, come to the Prayer!) or "As-salatu jami'ah!" (Gather for the Prayer!). However, such a call was not sufficient. Those living further away from the masjid had difficulty hearing the call and were thus late in joining the Prayers.

One day, our Prophet gathered his Companions and consulted with them about what kind of system they could develop to call all the believers to Prayer. The Companions offered many suggestions. Let's use a gong, or blow a horn; let's light a fire, they suggested. Our Prophet did not accept any of these suggestions, though. The meeting ended without them being able to reach an all-around decision. On one of these days, Abdullah ibn Zayd saw an interesting dream. When it was morning, he rushed to our Prophet and told him about his dream. "Last night in my dreams, a man came to me, dressed in green. He had a big bell in his hand. I asked him if he would sell the bell to me.

"What will you do with it," he asked.

"I will call people to Prayer with it," I answered.

"Would you like me to tell you of something that is much better," he asked in response.

"What is it," I replied. He turned in the direction of the *qiblah*, towards the Ka'ba, and started to recite,

"Allahu Akbar, Allahu Akbar, Allahu Akbar, Allahu Akbar (Allah is the Greatest, Allah is the Greatest, Allah is the Greatest, Allah is the Greatest)

Ashhadu an la ilaha illallah (I bear witness that there is no deity except the One Allah)

Ashhadu an la ilaha illallah (I bear witness that there is no deity except the One Allah)

Ashhadu anna Muhammadan Rasulullah (I bear witness that Muhammad is the Messenger of Allah)

Ashhadu anna Muhammadan Rasulullah (I bear witness that Muhammad is the Messenger of Allah)

Hayya alas-Salah, Hayya alas-Salah (Come to Prayer, come to Prayer)

Hayya alal-Falah, Hayya alal-Falah (Come to success, come to success (in this life and in the Hereafter))

Allahu Akbar, Allahu Akbar (Allah is the Greatest, Allah is the Greatest)

La ilaha illallah (There is no deity but the One Allah)"

Many other Companions had seen similar dreams that same night. Yet there was no difference in the call to Prayer that was taught to each one. Umar ibn al-Khattab was also among the ones that had seen the dream. After listening to all the Companions one by one, he turned to Abdullah ibn Zayd and said, "Teach Bilal what you have seen and let Bilal be the one to call the believers to Prayer, for his voice is stronger than yours." When it was Prayer time, Bilal climbed to the highest point in Medina and, with his strong voice, delivered the very first call to Prayer.

Our Prophet moved out of Abu Ayyub al-Ansari's home as soon as the construction of the Masjid an-Nabawi and the rooms next to it were completed. He and his daughters started living in the rooms that had been made for them. After a short period of time, Allah's Messenger and Abu Bakr's daughter Aisha's wedding took place. They had been engaged in Mecca, shortly before the Emigration, and their wedding had been postponed for later on. After the wedding, Aisha, may Allah be pleased with her, moved into the Blissful Household of Allah's Messenger. A new period in our Prophet's family life had begun.

Ashab as-Suffa
(The People of the Chamber)

The religion of Islam was now being taught to believers of all ages in the mosque of our Prophet. The Messenger of Allah would give daily lessons on the essentials of their religion to his Companions. Plus, there were about seventy young Muslims of limited means who lived in the courtyard of the masjid. These young believers had no home and no family. They would never leave our Prophet's side, would memorize his teachings and they would learn about Islam to the best of their ability. The place where they stayed was called Suffa and they were known as Ashab as-Suffa, or the People of the Chamber. Those living in Suffa would pray, read the Qur'an and study their lessons during the nights. During the daytime, they would carry water and gather wood to sell, and they would buy food with the money they earned.

The most honorable people in the world were raised in Suffa, the first Islamic school of all time, under the tutelage of our Prophet. Our Prophet would always think of them before thinking of himself and would also advise his Companions to look after and take care of them. In Suffa, these young believers were being raised so that they could be sent out to the four corners of the Arabian Peninsula to fulfill their duties later on. Teachers of the Qur'an and hadith for tribes that had newly become Muslim were chosen from among this very special group. There were to be the successors of our Prophet in terms of knowledge. Abu Hurayra, who has narrated the most hadith from our Prophet, was also from the Ashab as-Suffa.

A Promise of Unity

With the brotherhood that Allah's Messenger established in Medina, the believers had promised to support each other with both their fortunes and their lives. Through this practice the Messenger of Allah had laid the foundation for a powerful Islamic society. However, at that time, Medina had a population of approximately ten thousand people. The 1,500 Muslims lived together side-by-side with nearly 4,000 Jews and about 4,500 Arab polytheists. Thus, an order where the different groups of Medina could live together in harmony needed to be established.

The first task that the Messenger of Allah undertook was to have the borders of the city of Medina determined. The area within these borders was then named the Haram. Afterwards, a census was carried out in Medina for the very first time.

Allah's Messenger was restructuring Medina. Although it had only been a number of days since his arrival in Medina, the peaceful and secure environment that Allah's Messenger had established clearly manifested itself. It was unanimous among the people of Medina that in the event of a possible disagreement among themselves, our Prophet was surely the person to go to in order to resolve the problem.

If the city were to be attacked by enemies, it was essential for the people to unite into one. With this in mind, our Prophet decided to make certain covenants with the Jews and some of the tribes living in Medina. The first covenant in Medina was made between the tribes of Aws and Khazraj. In the end, our Prophet had taken over the rule of Medina through a written agreement. The covenant scripture started as follows:

"In the Name of Allah, the All-Merciful, the All-Compassionate...

This charter is a charter on the part of Muhammad who is the Messenger, concerning the Muslims and believers of the Quraysh and Yathrib, and other people who are bound to them, and those who have come later to accept the same terms and those who act in unison in matters of common defense. All who are stated above are a united people when faced against other people."

Following this statement, it was decided that all tribes would spread the good and benevolent throughout society while eliminating the bad and heinous. If despite all these precautions a disagreement were to take place, then the issue would be resolved by agreeing to the judgment passed by Allah and His Messenger.

The second was the treaty with the Jewish people. According to the agreement, in the face of battle, the Jewish people would contribute financially just as much as the Muslims. Medina would be under joint protection and working together would be the principle in defense. Both the Muslims and the Jews would be able to live freely according to their respective faiths. The Muslims would solve their problems according to the decrees of the Qur'an, the Word of Allah, and the Jewish people would solve their issues according to the decrees of their own holy scriptures, the Torah, and neither side would intervene in the judgments of the other. Should there be a disagreement despite all these provisions, again this would be solved according to the commandments of Allah and the arbitration of Prophet Muhammad, peace and blessings be upon him.

The Ka'ba, Our *Qiblah*,
Our Direction to Prayer

After the Emigration, for a period of sixteen months, our Prophet and the Muslims prayed facing the Al-Aqsa Mosque in Jerusalem, which was also the *qiblah*, or direction to Prayer, for the Jews. When in Mecca, the Messenger of Allah had prayed facing Jerusalem and the Ka'ba would also be standing in front of him. After emigrating to Medina, uniting the two was no longer possible. The Messenger of Allah missed facing the Ka'ba while praying. One day, he had said to the Archangel Gabriel, "O Gabriel! I truly wish for Allah the Almighty to turn my face from the *qiblah* of the Jews to the Ka'ba." Gabriel had answered, "Pray to your Lord, ask for this from Him."

Thereafter, our Prophet started raising his head to the skies every time he stood for Prayer. The verse, *"(Now the time has come, so) turn your face towards the Sacred Mosque. (And you, O believers,) turn your faces towards it wherever you are"* (al-Baqarah 2:144) was revealed. Allah the Almighty had appointed the Ka'ba as the new *qiblah* and from then on, the Muslims started to pray facing the Ka'ba. These new developments had happened to fall on a Monday in the beginning of the seventeenth month after the Emigration. Our Prophet had happened to be in the Banu Salama neighborhood that day. It was the time for

Noon Prayer and so, he stood in Prayer together with his Companions in the *masjid* there. They had prayed only two *rakah*s, or units, and the command to turn towards the Ka'ba came to him while still in Prayer. The Messenger of Allah turned and the congregation behind him turned as well. It was after this incident that the masjid in the Banu Salama was named, "The *Masjid* with Two *Qiblah*s."

Two months later, in the second of the holy months, the month of Shaban, the fasting in Ramadan was deemed obligatory, or *fard*.

The First Victory

The Muslims had endured many hardships and suffering in the fifteen-year period after the coming of the first revelation in the cave of Hira. Some had found themselves under great oppression and torture so that they would reject their new faith while others found no other choice than to abandon their homes and countries. Some had fled to Abyssinia and some had been forced to emigrate to Medina. In Medina, however, the Muslims had now formed a unity. Islam was spreading even further with each passing day, and the believers were growing stronger by the minute. The Qurayshi non-believers had grown even more furious and desperate against Allah the Almighty. Infuriated at not being able to stop him from emigrating to Medina, they grew even more persistent in denying the Messenger of Allah. "From now on, Muhammad will be able to spread his religion freely there and the number of people believing him will increase day by day," was the thought that ate away their brains just like the woodworm had eaten away their boycott document. Once again they were gathered at Daru'n-Nadwa, the place where they always got together when reaching important decisions. The buzzing of the crowd was pierced by Abu Jahl's words; "Muhammad slipped away from our hands. What's more, the number of those gathering around him are increasing day by day. Fortunately, the things belonging to the ones who fled to Medina are still here."

"What are you trying to say Abu Jahl? Make it clear," one called out from the crowd. With revenge and animosity oozing out from between his teeth, Abu Jahl cried out, "We are not only going to wipe out Muhammad, we are going to wipe out him and all those who believe in him."

"And how are we going to do that," asked another.

"By war! They have no idea about combat. Besides, they've left behind whatever possessions they have. We can prepare a great army after selling the believers' belongings. Then we can charge against them and kill them all," exclaimed Abu Jahl.

Everyone's eyes at the meeting had lit up with joy. Indeed, the people of Medina, being a people of agriculture, did not know much about combat. What's more, they had neither an army nor the weapons to equip that army with. The non-believers, on the other hand, were putting forth great effort to prepare an army that was superior both number and weapon-wise. All the property left behind that had belonged to the believers who had left Mecca, every single piece was plundered. The non-believers were going to load all the possessions onto a caravan heading to Damascus, sell them and were going to prepare their army with the profit they made.

This caravan, led by Abu Sufyan, had gone to Damascus and was coming back with its unjust profit. Our Prophet, who had been informed of all that had been happening, planned an intervention to this caravan, with Allah's permission. In this way, they were both going to intimidate the non-believers and also take back the money that rightfully belonged to the Muslims, the true owners of the possessions.

When Abu Sufyan learned that our Prophet was going to set out in pursuit of the caravan, he immediately changed his route and took the road that was further away from Medina and closer to the coast. He also sent a messenger to Mecca, to inform them of the situation. When the messenger reached Mecca his heart was about to burst from the excitement and rush. He spoke to the crowd of people that gathered around him, full of curiosity.

"Muhammad had raided the caravan and has taken over all the goods," he said.

In reality, though, our Prophet was just following the caravan at that point. Upon the words of the messenger, the leaders of Mecca gave orders for the army to be prepared right away. Whatever was needed for a battle was brought together in a very short period of time. Manpower, horses, camels, weapons and money... The non-believers had not wasted any time and had set out from Mecca with an army of 1,000, whereas there were only a mere 300 gathered around the Messenger of Allah. Even worse, the Muslims had very few horses and their weapons were terribly insufficient.

The army led by Abu Jahl and the caravan led by Abu Sufyan met each other somewhere along the way. Abu Sufyan said, "As you can see, none of the goods have been damaged. I managed to escape their pursuit. There is no need for battle. Come, let us go back now."

"What are you saying Abu Sufyan? We have come all this way from Mecca with such a magnificent army. We cannot return without destroying Muhammad and his friends," roared Abu Jahl!

Abu Sufyan was much calmer about the situation. "Didn't you come here to save the caravan? You have seen that the caravan is safe. There's no longer a need to fight," he repeated.

"Not at all, there are plenty of reasons for us to fight. Until we have gotten rid of Muhammad there will be plenty of reason for us to fight," roared Abu Jahl once again.

This time Abu Sufyan's answer was crystal clear. "My duty was to return the caravan safe and sound back to Mecca, and that is exactly what I will do. I am not coming with you to fight, I am going to Mecca," he said.

As he ordered the caravan to take up speed once again, he looked over at Abu Jahl and the others with him and said, "You will do nothing but perish yourselves." With that he mounted his horse and rode on towards Mecca.

Meanwhile, our Prophet had been informed that the polytheist army had started out of Mecca, and so he had found it suitable that they wait for them near the water wells at Badr. When the Islamic army reached the water nearest Badr, our Prophet consulted with the Medinan Muslims on where they should set up the army headquarters. Hubab knew the water wells in the surroundings very well. He shared his opinion, saying, "O Messenger of Allah! This is not a very suitable location to settle down. Let us go to the water closest to our enemies. Let us dig a pool there and fill it with water. Then, let us close up all the other wells. This way, we can drink water from our own pool during the battle, and they will be left without water."

Our Prophet and his Companions liked this idea very much. The plan was implemented in exactly the same way. They settled down and set up the headquarters right next to the water well they had spoken of. That night, in his tent, the Messenger of Allah prayed until the morning light and supplicated to his Lord, saying, "O my Gracious Lord! There the Quraysh stands before us with all their self-esteem and pomp. They dare to challenge You, and they accuse Your Messenger of being a liar. My Lord, I ask of You to grant us the victory which You have promised us, against them. My Lord, early tomorrow morning, rub their noses against the dirt in the battlefield!"

Meanwhile, it had started raining in Badr, as a kind of messenger of mercy before the start of the battle. Together with the rain, the Almighty Allah had also sent down a peaceful and relaxing sleepiness over the Muslims, and they had all fallen into a sweet slumber behind the shelter of the trees. This sweet slumber had been a kind of Divine aid for the Muslims so that they could forget the fatigue and hardships they had endured up until then and become refreshed and energetic for the following day. With the same rain, the non-believers found themselves struggling with many hardships difficult to overcome, having trouble even walking as they sank into the mud and dirt.

In the morning of that night, our Prophet gathered his Companions at Badr and lined them up in rows, ready for battle, before the polytheist army even had a chance to arrive and get settled.

Meanwhile, a wind, unlike any other they had seen before, passed by. A second and third gust of wind followed shortly after and passed by. With the first wind, the Archangel Gabriel, with the second, the Archangel Michael, and with the third, the Archangel Israfil, upon them be peace, took their places next to our Prophet, each accompanied by a thousand Archangels. The Archangels had wrapped their heads in green, yellow and red turbans, leaving one end of the cloth flowing down their backs. There were signs made of wool adorning the foreheads of their horses.

Despite all the efforts of some individuals in the Meccan army about not wanting to fight against their own brothers and relatives, the desire for revenge and feeling of hatred from Abu Jahl and those like him had won out in the end. When the efforts to prevent battle had proved futile, the first thing the Messenger of Allah did was turn towards the *qiblah* and perform two *rakah*s of Prayer in supplication to Allah the Almighty, for Him to help them overcome the enemy who outnumbered them greatly. Then he opened his blessed hands and pleaded to his Lord, "O my Gracious Lord! Grant us that which You have promised us! O my Almighty Allah! If you are to destroy this mere handful of believers, then there will be no one left in this world to worship and glorify You!"

Just then, because his hands were raised to the sky, a part of his dress slid off his shoulder. Abu Bakr put it back in place and did not leave our Prophet's side. The Messenger's supplications had grown so intense that Abu Bakr couldn't stop himself from saying,

"O Messenger of Allah! All this supplication to your Lord is enough! He will, without a doubt, fulfill His promise to you!"

It was at that moment that Allah the Almighty sent down this verse to our Prophet; "When you were imploring your Lord for help (as a special mercy), and He responded to you: "I will help you with a thousand Archangels, coming host after host. "Upon this, our Prophet turned to his faithful Companion and said, "I have glad tidings! O Abu Bakr! Allah's help has arrived! That over there is Gabriel! Atop the Naq Hill, holding the rein of his horse, equipped with his weapons and coat of armor! Ready for battle!"

They could hear more neighing of horses and clinking of swords than there actually was in the valley of Badr now. In such an atmosphere, the strength of the opposing forces had gradually decreased while the strength of our Prophet and his respected Companions gradually increased. These tidings had spread throughout the Companions in a very short period of time and faces shone with delight. The Messenger of Allah had one more piece of glad tidings to share with his Companions. He turned to them and said, "I feel as though I can see the very point in which each non-believer will be killed by the end of today!"

After a series of fighting and rigorous battles against each other, the Muslims wiped out the enemies of Islam and gained a glorious victory. There was nothing left of the Qurayshi army in the valley of Badr other than the lifeless bodies laying in the battlefield and the captives tied up and waiting in one corner. The Quraysh had come all the way from Mecca to Badr with such high hopes, and now they had no other choice than to go back with disappointment and casualties. Abu Jahl and many other Qurayshi leaders lost their lives in this battle named the Battle of Badr. Aside from the seventy non-believers who had been killed in the war, seventy more were held captive. There had also been a total of fourteen martyrs in the believers' side. Though they had gained victory over the non-believers, still, a sorrow had fallen over Badr on account of the fourteen martyrs. Allah's Messenger himself led the Funeral Prayer for those who came to Badr and who became the first ones among them all to be blessed with the honor of martyrdom. He prayed for them and accompanied them in their last journey.

Because this had been their first battle ever fought, what they would do about the captives was going to be a whole new experience for them. There was no other similar practice which would serve as an example to resolve the situation about the captives. To make it worse, no Divine command had been sent to show them the proper way, either. The Messenger of Allah immediately called his Companions together so that they could discuss and consult each other on what to do about the situation. He said, "What do you think we should do about the captives? Even if they were your brothers yesterday, today, Allah has made them dependent of the decision that you will come to."

As an outcome of the consultation, the general opinion was that the captives be freed in exchange for ransom money. Those who did not have the means to pay the ransom would be freed in exchange for teaching ten Muslims to read and write. Still there were those who could neither pay the ransom nor knew how to read and write. The Muslims did not leave them stranded like that, though. They too would be set free on the condition that, from that day on, they would not speak badly of Islam or help, in any way, those fighting against the Muslims. Many people from both Mecca and Medina became Muslim after this incident.

After Badr

After the victory of the Muslims at Badr, the Meccan non-believers had grown even more hateful and revengeful towards the believers. Tragedy had hit almost every home in Mecca after the great battle. Mecca was now after revenge. People were taking oath after oath for its sake. In fact, there were even some in Medina that had been disturbed by the victory of the Muslims at Badr. They were none other than the polytheists who secretly supported the Quraysh and the Jews who did not like the thought of superiority of anyone else besides themselves. The Muslims, on the other hand, connected even deeper to one another after this glorious victory that had been granted to them from their Lord.

That year, for the very first time, they had fasted during the month of Ramadan and were going to celebrate their first festival, Eid al-Fitr. Also, the special Tarawih Prayers were performed for the very first time, and the charity of fast-breaking was deemed necessary for a practicing believer. At the same time, during the month of Ramadan of the second year after Emigration, alms-giving was deemed obligatory while sacrificing an animal in the month of Dhu al-Hijjah and performing the Eid (Festival) Prayer were deemed necessary. It was during these days of bliss and serenity that the Muslims lined up behind the Messenger of Allah and performed the Eid Prayer for the first time.

Again it was on one of these days that Ali, son of our Prophet's uncle Abu Talib, was wed to our Prophet's daughter, Fatima. A year later, their son, Hasan, came into this world. His birth made our beloved Prophet truly happy.

Towards a New Battle

Three years had passed after the Emigration. The Quraysh, unable to forget the great blow that had struck them at Badr, had prepared a new army with help and support from the surrounding tribes. They had started out from Mecca towards Medina with the thought of taking revenge from the Muslims. Our Prophet learned about the situation thanks to a letter that his uncle, noble Abbas, sent to him from Mecca. A short while later, the Messenger of Allah was also informed of the fact that the Meccan army consisted of three thousand people. The polytheists were advancing towards Medina with three thousand camels, two hundred horses and great determination. Abu Sufyan was the commander of the army. Khalid ibn Walid was the commander of the horseman and Abu Jahl's son, Ikrima, was helping him.

The Meccan army had come very close to Uhud and was waiting there with the thought of destroying Medina all together. The Messenger of Allah came together with his Companions in order to consult with them about how they should take action against the recent developments. First, they considered the information they had on the Meccan army. Especially the Companions who had become Muslim after the battle of Badr were for confronting them and fighting. However, our Prophet thought that it would be more convenient to defend the city without leaving it. He had shared with some of his Companions a dream he had seen which he interpreted to mean that some of his Companions would be martyred in this battle. For this reason he was in support of defense rather than offense. Despite this, the Messenger of Allah also wanted instill the concept of consultation, which was one of Allah's commands, into the society of the believers. Seeing that the majority favored the strategy of fighting outside of Medina, he conformed according to the general preference and decided they meet the Meccan army outside of Medina.

The Day of Uhud

The morning of the battle had come at last. Seven hundred Muslims were standing against a polytheist army of three thousand people. That morning, after the Prayer, the Messenger of Allah sat with his Companions and talked with them lengthily. He advised the believers to behave accordingly to the holy book of Allah, to be mindful of what is permitted and what is not, to be patient and dignified at all times. He commanded them to be unified, work as one, and be cautious of the enemy at all times. Then he asked that his Companions get ready for battle. He personally lined them up in rows and said to them, "No one shall start fighting until I have given permission to do so!"

The Meccan army, full of excessive self-confidence, was waiting for them at Uhud. Khalid ibn Walid was standing on the right side of the army, with his two-hundred horsemen. The Messenger of Allah chose fifty archers and appointed Abdullah ibn Jubayr as their commander.

The he pointed to the horsemen in the polytheist army and firmly instructed them,

"Keep these horsemen away from us; do not let them come from behind and besiege us! Even if, for a moment, it seems as though the victory is on our side, do not abandon your positions! Make sure that we are not attacked from your side. Take your positions and do not leave them for any reason whatsoever! Even if you see that we have defeated them and you see us among their soldiers, do not leave your positions! Even if you see crows hovering over us eating away at our flesh, do not leave your positions unless I have sent word to you! If you see that we are being killed, do not attempt to come to our aid; do not rush to our defense and support! Shoot them with your arrows instead because horses cannot advance when they have arrows being shot at them! And never forget that, as long as you stay in your positions, we will be the conquering side."

After Allah's Messenger prayed, "O my Gracious Allah! I make the effort and attack in Your Name only, and only in Your Name do I advance onto the enemies. My struggle with the enemy is for Your sake only! You are my sole power of support and what a wonderful Protector You are," the battle had finally begun.

It was a ruthless and fearsome battle. Ali and our Prophet's uncle, Hamza, had gone in through one end of the non-believer army and had come out through the other end. The other Companions were also fighting courageously, shouting periodic cries of exaltation to their Lord. Before long, the non-believer army was dispersed and had started to retreat. The clinking of the swords had decreased and a kind of chase had started, so to speak. The polytheists, whose unity had been shattered, were running to save their lives.

On that day of battle, the mounted troops of the Meccan army attempted to attack at three different occasions, and each time they were driven back by the attack of the archers. The horses were unable to advance against the flood of arrows raining on them, just like our Prophet had said. The reason that our Prophet had so insistently warned the fifty archers to not leave their positions was indeed this very fact. However, seeing that the Muslims were chasing the non-believers, the archers atop Mount Uhud left their positions, thinking that they had won the battle. The mounted troops of the polytheist army noticed that the archers had left their position. Without wasting any time, they rushed over and besieged the Muslim army from behind. Without having the arrows raining over them, the polytheist horsemen had taken advantage of the opportunity for easy attack. Thus the Islam army found itself in between the enemy just when it was least expected. When the non-believers who had been running away noticed what had just happened, they turned around and came back to attack as well. Shouts of, "For the sake of Uzza!" and "In the name of Hubal!" rang in their ears. The believers had unexpectedly found themselves in a very tight situation. What seemed like a small act of neglect was about to change the course of everything.

The main goal for the non-believers was, without a doubt, the Messenger of Allah, and, even amongst all this chaos, they had him especially in target. A non-believer named Utba ibn Abi Waqqas had thrown four stones one after the other, and one of them had struck our Prophet's blessed face. As a result, his lower right tooth had broken and his blessed lips had also been wounded. Taking opportunity of the disorder, the non-believers were attacking non-stop. Arrows and stones were raining over the Messenger of Allah. For a moment, Ibn Qamiah's voice could be heard.

"Take this! I am Ibn Qamiah," he was shouting, and he was attacking Allah's Messenger with one blow after another. Upon this, our Prophet turned towards him and responded, "Let Allah himself take care of you."

In the face of another danger, the Messenger of Allah called out, "Who will fight against these?" The response was from a high-pitched but strong voice calling out, "I will, O Messenger of Allah!"

The voice belonged to Nasiba bint Ka'b. This self-sacrificing woman had mounted her horse and rode to Uhud, to our Prophet's side, and she was fighting to protect him. Upon hearing the cry of Ibn Qamiah's challenge against the Messenger of Allah, she and Mus'ab ibn Umayr decided to advance onto him and eliminate him with a few blows with their swords. However, Ibn Qamiah had put on two coats of armor that day and So, the strikes from Nasiba bint Ka'b's sword could not finish the task.

Mus'ab ibn Umayr was carrying the banner of the Messenger of Allah that day, and he was fighting like a lion. The scattering of the Muslims, for an instant, had saddened him deeply. He was fighting with all his might, with the banner in one hand and his sword in the other. Meanwhile, the non-believer Ibn Qamiah had taken an oath to kill our beloved Prophet. Mus'ab looked very much like our Prophet when inside his coat of armor. So, Ibn Qamiah found Mus'ab and stood against him to fight. After a fearsome struggle between the two, Mus'ab was martyred. After his martyrdom, the banner of Islam did not fall to the ground. An Archangel, in the form of Mus'ab, carried the banner of the Muslims in his place.

Ibn Qamiah, on the other hand, thought that he had killed Allah's Messenger. He returned to the Quraysh and cried out in joy, "I killed Muhammad!" These words echoed throughout Uhud. This news devoured whatever strength the Muslims had left. There were ones who dropped their swords and cried out frantically when they heard of the news echoing throughout:

Amidst the turmoil, Ka'b ibn Malik was the first to see and announce to the believers that the Messenger of Allah was living. He cried with a strong voice, "I saw the Messenger of Allah with these very eyes; there was blood streaking down from under his headpiece but he was alive! O Muslim men and women! Good tidings to you! The Messenger of Allah is right over there," and announced that our Prophet had not been killed to everyone that he came across.

With these cries of joy, Uhud had found life once again. Everyone turned to where the voice came from and life had filled Uhud once again.

Meanwhile, our Prophet's headpiece had broken to pieces and two of its rings had sunk into his cheeks. One of his teeth had been broken, and his lips and face were wounded and bleeding. This situation brought unbearable pain to our Prophet's Companions. Blood was oozing down the face of the Messenger of Allah, for whose sake they were willing to sacrifice their lives. The beloved Prophet of compassion, on the other hand, had opened his hands to the skies and was praying for those who had wounded his head and broken his tooth.

"O my Gracious Lord! Show my people the rightful path! For they do not know," he prayed. He was so full of mercy and compassion, even towards those who wanted to kill him.

There was another great sorrow that awaited our beloved Prophet on that day of Uhud. His uncle, Hamza, had been martyred by a slave named Wahshi. Hamza had been known as "the lion of Allah" when he was alive, and he handed in his soul as "the master of martyrs."

The Companions of our Prophet were trying to protect Allah's Messenger with all their might, on one hand, and were retreating towards and gathering at the foothills of the mountain, on the other. This was the first step in turning the battle at Uhud to the advantage of the believers. Following that very challenging and tough period in the battle, Allah the Almighty sent down a feeling of Divine peace and serenity over the Islam army to assure that the believers both reach a state of inner comfort and physical rest. The Archangel, who had taken over Mus'ab ibn Umayr's duty of carrying the banner of Islam after he had been martyred, continued to wave the banner of Islam in the air at Uhud.

Both sides had suffered great casualties, and the commander of the Meccan army, Abu Sufyan, found it dangerous to attack the Muslims once again. The retreat of the Muslims towards the foothills of Mount Uhud, and the way they gathered together has startled him a bit. Therefore, he called his army to return back to Mecca in order to, at least, not harm the victory they had achieved up to that point.

As Abu Sufyan and his soldiers were starting to turn back, the Messenger of Allah wanted to be certain that they were not planning something evil against them. For he was worried that they might enter Medina to harm the women and children on their way back. Thus, he called his leading Companions to his side and instructed them to follow the polytheist army.

"If they mount their camels when leaving, this means they will leave without committing any harm. However, if they leave the camels and mount their horses, this means that they are aiming for Medina! And this would mean none other than explicit plunder. If you notice such an intention, then we will all unite and advance onto them," he said.

After being instructed by the Messenger of Allah, the Respected Companions started their pursuit of the enemy. They were so close that they could even hear the things that the polytheists were talking amongst themselves. A group of polytheists wanted to plunder Medina while they had the chance, but others, like Safwan ibn Umayya, said, "Don't even let the thought cross your mind! Don't you see how they've come back together and how fearlessly they walk into the eyes of death! There is no way that we can reach Muhammad before killing them all. Let's get out of here before turning our victory into a pathetic defeat."

And so, the Meccan army mounted their camels for the long journey and set off on the road. The fearlessness and determination of the believers in honor of the cause they believed in had discouraged the Meccan army and forced them to leave Uhud with a rush.

When the non-believers decided not to take the risk of continuing in battle and retreated out of Uhud, the Respected Companions of our Prophet walked back to the battlefield among the bodies of the dead and wounded. The wounded were to be taken and the martyrs were to be trusted over to Mount Uhud. Testifying on account of his Companions who sacrificed their lives for the sake of Allah the Almighty, our beloved Prophet declared, "The Messenger of Allah testifies that in the Day of Judgment you will also be martyrs in the eyes of Allah!"

Then, he turned to the Muslims and said, "O people! Come here to visit them on different occasions! Send greetings to them. I swear to Allah, whose Hand of Power bears possession to myself, that they will accept and respond to the greetings of every believer that greets them until the Day of Judgment."

After the Muslims returned to Medina, every believer took sanctuary in their own home and started to take care of their wounds. Before long, Bilal shouted the call for the Evening Prayer. Upon hearing the call, the believers gathered in the masjid and performed the Prayer altogether. The Night Prayer was also performed in congregation in the *masjid*. The Battle of Uhud, which had started in the morning of that Saturday, ended by the Evening Prayer of that very same day.

The believers retreated into their homes to rest and heal their wounds that Saturday night, and on Sunday morning, with the call to Prayer from Bilal, they all gathered again in the Masjid an-Nabawi.

The Messenger of Allah was not sure whether the nonbelievers were going to come back or not because they were returning from the battle with nothing in their hands. It was highly likely that they change their minds while on their way back, and come back to Medina to attack once again. They had to prevent such a possibility from arising. Also, they needed to let everyone know that Medina was the authority once again after the battle of Uhud. Surely, a short while later, our Prophet's worries were justified. After having advanced a bit on their journey, indeed, the Quraysh evaluated their situation. Talking among themselves,, they decided that it was wrong for them to return empty-handed and that they needed to attack Medina once again, this time to wipe the Muslims out altogether. They had fought but now had nothing in their hands to show that they had won the battle.

Some of them insisted that they go back to fight, but not everyone agreed. Safwan ibn Umayya expressed his own opinion,

"O my tribe! Do not dare to try this! Right now they are much more furious with us than ever before. I am afraid that they will gather up those who were not with them at Uhud, and they will come to attack us all together. The best thing for you to do is be content with what you have in your hands and go back without losing any time. For I am afraid that if you do attack them once again, you will also lose what you already have!"

When the Messenger of Allah heard of this news, he first consulted Abu Bakr and Umar. They decided to follow the non-believers to keep an eye on them.

Meanwhile, despite the fact that there were some who insisted on going back to Mecca, the majority had agreed on the idea to attack Medina once again, and the Meccan army was just getting ready to take off. Just then, news that the Muslims were coming after them reached the army. Seeing that they had been mistaken in thinking that they had heavily beat the Muslims, the non-believers started to panic when they learned that they were being pursued, and so decided to return to Mecca.

Even when full of fear, the polytheists did not pass an opportunity to supposedly challenge the believers. They sent word to the Messenger of Allah, through a caravan they ran across on the road, saying, "After gathering up our strength once again, we are going to come back and wipe out you and your Companions!"

When this news reached him, our Prophet merely said, "Allah is sufficient for us and what a wonderful support He is!"

After intimidating the enemy, the Muslims returned to Medina having bandaged the wounds from Uhud. Thus, the victors of Uhud were the Islam army once again.

An Attempt at Assassination

The thought of still not being able to take the revenge of Badr and not being able to take advantage of the opportunity at Uhud, bothered the Meccan polytheists greatly. They had not yet given up on the thought of killing the Messenger of Allah. One day, Abu Sufyan gathered a group of young men around him and asked, "Isn't there a valiant one among you who will finish off Muhammad? Just look, he's walking around free of worries while we're suffering in anguish!"

However, not one out of the group had the courage to step forward. Abu Sufyan had no other choice than to return to his house empty-handed. A while later, there was a knocking on Abu Sufyan's door. When he opened the door, the young Bedouin standing at the door said, "If you give me your word and behave generously towards my requests, I will go and kill him! I know these kinds of jobs very well."

Abu Sufyan was overjoyed. He had found just the man he was looking for. He gave the young man as many goods and property as he pleased and they made an agreement. Then he gave him strict orders to not tell anyone else of their agreement.

The young Bedouin set off on his journey in the dark of the night, and after a six-day journey he finally reached Medina. He found our Prophet by asking those he came across along the way. He was able to come very close to our Prophet. Meanwhile, our beloved Prophet sensed what his intentions were. He shared his feelings with those around him, but he also assured them that Allah would not permit him to do what he came there to do. The young Bedouin asked, "Which one of you is the son of Abdul Muttalib?"

Allah's Messenger responded, "I am the son of Abdul Muttalib!"

Upon the answer, the young Bedouin wanted to draw closer to our Prophet, as though he were going to secretly tell him something. Usayd ibn Khudayr sensed his bad intention. Remembering the words he had heard from our Prophet he called out, "Stay away from the Messenger of Allah," and pulled the young Bedouin from his dress.

Just then, the dagger that the young man was hiding in his waist was exposed. Seeing that his intention was out in the open the young Bedouin was filled with fear. He was asking for mercy from the Messenger of Allah whom he was trying to kill just seconds ago.

Allah's Messenger turned to the young Bedouin and said, "Tell me the truth! Who are you and why did you come here? If you tell the truth, this will only bring you goodness and aid. Even if you are to lie, in the end, I will find out the things that you hide from me!"

The young Bedouin asked, "Am I safe? Can I trust you?" Our beloved Prophet's response was, "Yes, you truly are safe."

Following this, the young man told of everything that happened to him, starting from Mecca. That night he stayed under custody in Usayd ibn Khudayr's home. The next day, the Messenger of Allah called him to his side and said to him,

"Now, you are free to go wherever you like. Or, you can choose to do something that will bring you much more goodness." The young man asked right away, "What is this more auspicious deed?"

The Messenger of Allah replied, "For you to testify that there is no deity but Allah and that I am His Messenger."

The mercy of our Prophet had touched the young Bedouin deeply. With serenity in his heart, he declared, "I bear witness that there is no deity but Allah and, without a doubt, you are His Messenger." Then he turned to Allah's Messenger and said, "I swear to you, O Muhammad! You are a man of utmost compassion! From the very moment that I saw you, my mind flew out of my head, my hands and arms were tied and I had no idea what I was doing! Then, how quickly you realized what my real intention was. No one else knew of my plan, and, even if they had, there was no one to bring the news to you! That was when I realized that you are truly being protected against all evil. You represent the truth, and those following Abu Sufyan are nothing but soldiers of Satan!"

The Messenger of Allah smiled after hearing these words. One more person, who had set out to kill him, had found peace in his atmosphere.

Conveying of the Message
Continues

After the battle of Uhud, in the fourth year after the Emigration, the Muslims living in Medina had grown much more powerful. The enemies of Islam had also grown much more dangerous, and were getting ready to attack every chance they got. Our Prophet continued to take defense and protection precautions against the enemies, on one hand, and teach people about Islam and invite others to embrace faith, on the other. The area of conveying the message and guiding the believers to a stronger faith grew wider with each passing day as they reached new people and faces. They did whatever they needed to do, whether it be learning a new language or sending a messenger to a new place.

That year Ali and Fatima's second son was born. The birth of his grandson, Husayn, had made our Prophet very happy. When speaking of his beloved grandsons Hasan and Husayn, he would say, "They are my two sweet-smelling flowers in this world."

A Treacherous Offer

I t was the fifth year after the Emigration. The enemies of Islam could in no way bring themselves to accept the spread of the religion. They decided to organize another battle against the Muslims. A much greater army was to be prepared. This time their goal was to wipe out the Muslims altogether. They were going to attack Medina, the city which smelled of roses, and they were going to slay all the believers one by one. This time it was the Jews who were provoking the Quraysh. They came to Mecca with this proposal, "We are together with you in this war against Muhammad. Let us come shoulder-to-shoulder and uproot him from the face of the earth!"

The Quraysh grew very fond of this treacherous plan. After all, this had been their sole desire for so many years. They had in no way gotten over their defeat at Badr, and were in constant watch for an opportunity to take their revenge. Abu Sufyan's reply to the Jews was as follows,

"The most charming person for us if the one who will work with us and help us in defeating Muhammad."

Seeing that working together against the Muslims was a golden opportunity for both sides, they decided on a time they would later meet and went their separate ways.

Breaking away from the Quraysh, the Jews were not set on being content with only that much evil. They travelled to all of the other Arabian tribes, one-by-one, with the same offer. They set a date with every tribe they agreed with and told them to be prepared by that time. They had convinced nearly all of the tribes to fight against the Messenger of Allah and the believers.

Days went by and the time came. An army of four thousand soldiers, commanded by Abu Sufyan, took off from Mecca and advanced towards Medina. There were a total of three hundred horses and one thousand five hundred camels in the army. Upon hearing this, the other tribes, too, started taking action and came to join Abu Sufyan's army in flocks. Before long, the number of these non-believers obsessed with revenge had reached ten thousand.

The Defense of the City of the Rose

The Messenger of Allah had become aware of these latest developments beforehand. He came together with his Companions in consultation so they could decide the plan of action they needed to take. Even though the Muslims did not want to fight, the Quraysh had come together and were coming their way. They needed to find a way to overcome this tribulation. Our beloved Prophet asked his Companions one by one on what action they thought needed to be taken. Should they stay in Medina and weaken the enemy by scattering them throughout the streets of the city? Or would it be more convenient to come out of Medina, fight chest to chest in the battlefield and push back the enemy that way?

Everyone put their opinion forward, but most of which were spoken were risky. Just then, one of the Companions, Salman al-Farisi, put forth an idea. "O Messenger of Allah, in the land of Fars, when faced with the danger of raids by horsemen, we would dig trenched surrounding us and thus would protect ourselves!"

This offer was accepted with contentment by both our Prophet and the Respected Companions. A great trench was to be dug surrounding Medina, the City of the Rose, and the city was to be protected in this way.

Later on, the location for the trench was determined. Because the surroundings of Medina made it difficult to be surpassed by armies, the enemies could only approach from the relatively more favorable northern face of the city. And that was exactly where the trench was going to be dug. The area was divided amongst the Companions and the digging operation started right away. The operation needed to be completed before the Meccan army arrived. Our beloved Prophet also worked alongside his Companions. Everyone was so locked into their task that they knew no such thing as getting tired. All hearts were beating with the same excitement for the same goal. The task of digging started right after the Morning Prayer and continued until sunset, and at nights, the Companions retreated into their homes to rest.

The Messenger of Allah had devoted himself so much to this task that sometimes he would be digging the trench with a pickax, other times he would be carrying the dirt on his back and other times he would be throwing over the dirt with a shovel in his hand. Once, he had grown so tired that he had sat down in a corner to rest for a bit. He had rested his cheek on a stone and had fallen asleep just like that. This situation did not slip Abu Bakr and Umar's notice. They immediately came over to where he was sleeping and told the others to move away and not make any noise so that our Prophet could rest for a while. Our beloved Prophet's sleep didn't last long, though. Before long, he jumped out of his sleep.

"Why didn't you wake me up? I wish you had woken me up earlier," he said regretfully. He picked up his pickax and continued digging from where he left off.

Meanwhile, he was also praying for his Companions and referring those who had troubled them in such a way to the mercy of Allah.

The digging of the trench was completed at the end of six days. There was now a long and wide obstacle in between the city of Medina and the non-believers. The Meccan army had reached Mount Uhud at the same time the Muslims had finished the digging of the trench.

The Bewilderment at the Trench

The Muslim army consisted of a total of three thousand people. With their backs to the mountains and facing the trench, they started awaiting the enemy. It hadn't been long until the Meccan army of ten-thousand showed itself from across. As they were moving forward with much self-confidence and avidity, the great trench they saw before them took them by surprise and bewilderment. Never before had they seen such a defense strategy. Thinking that the trench was only in front of them, they started moving to the left and right. When they saw that all possible entrances to Medina were surrounded with the trench they realized that this was a futile effort. What great disappointment it was that they were not even able to enter the city whose people they had been planning to slay one by one and destroy altogether!

When they realized they would not be able to enter Medina, they settled in the area across the trench and started to wait. This stressful wait went on for days. The non-believers made many attempts to get across the trench. They threw arrows, spears, and stones, but whatever they did, they were not able to reach across to Medina. At last, they decided to cross through the weakest part of the trench. One group of polytheists started crossing over to the believers' side from a narrow pathway that they discovered. They thought they would be able to endanger the Muslims greatly. However, things didn't turn out as they expected. Seeing that the non-believers were crossing the trench, the Muslims rushed to that point to stop the others from coming in. When one of the soldiers among them lost his life, the other polytheists turned back without wasting any time. After this incident, they decided to attack all together, without leaving any one behind. And so they did, but even though they worked so hard, they were not able to reach their goal. In the end, they had no choice but to retreat.

Divine Aid

The persistent waiting of the non-believers continued on. After seeing the Archangel Gabriel appear beside them, our Prophet turned to his Companions and repeated three times, "Pay attention. Rejoice with the glad tidings from Allah the Almighty."

As soon as he finished his sentence, a great storm broke out in the area where the non-believer army had settled. Tents broke loose and flew away from where they had been tied down. Nothing was visible beyond an arm's length. The sky had darkened. The polytheists, who had already been shivering, got even colder with the storm, and now they were completely wretched. They were trying to tie the ropes and hammer in the poles of the tents that had been torn apart, but each time, a new storm broke out and they couldn't find the opportunity.

The gust of wind that Allah the Almighty had sent down in their aid filled the non-believers' eyes with sand and left them in unbearable pain! After this last incident, the only thing left for the polytheist army to do was to go back to where they came from. By morning, there was not even a single enemy soldier left by the trench.

Turning to his Companions our beloved Prophet said, "From now on, they will not be the ones to come at us during a battle. We will be the decisive force in the battlefields!"

Then he ordered for everyone to return to Medina. Thus, this battle, which was named the Battle of the Trench afterwards and which had taken a period of nearly one month, had finally ended.

The Dream of the *Umra*
(Minor Pilgrimage)

It was the sixth year after the Emigration. The Messenger of Allah and his Companions had missed the Ka'ba greatly. At around the same time, our Prophet had seen a dream which he had shared with his Companions. Our Prophet had gone to the House of Allah in his dream, and they had fulfilled their duty of *umra*, or minor pilgrimage. In the continuation of that same dream, Allah's Messenger had been presented with the keys to the Ka'ba. When it was morning and our beloved Prophet shared the dream with his Companions, Medina filled with joy. The thought of fulfilling their longing to the Ka'ba pleased everyone very much.

Preparations were tended to right away. Because their goal was not to fight but to worship they only took their tiny swords with them in order to protect themselves from the wild animals. They also had sheep and camels with them, which they were bringing along as sacrificial animals. They set off on the road on a Monday. When they reached Dhul-Hulayfa they dressed in their garments of consecration and continued towards Mecca whilst chanting the *talbiya*, meaning glorification and acceptance of servitude.

The Meccans had been informed that the Messenger of Allah was coming towards Mecca with his Companions in order to perform their *umra*. A state of fear and panic took over them. Even if they were not coming to fight, the Meccans had no intention of letting the Muslims enter the city.

The believers had reached a place called Hudaybiya. The weather was quite hot and the people had grown thirsty. Allah's Messenger found a well with a bit of water in it and settled there. There was no other water well near there any way. It was time for the Afternoon Prayer, and the Messenger of Allah was making ablution using the ewer he held in his hand. His Companions had gathered around him as he was making ablution and were watching him. The Messenger of Allah asked, "What is going on?"

"O Messenger of Allah! We have no water to drink or make ablution with except the water you hold in your hand," they replied.

Hearing this, our Prophet asked for them to first pour the water in the ewer into one big container. Then he dipped his blessed fingers into the container and started praying. Then he said, "Go on, take it! In the Name of Allah."

Allah the Almighty had granted a miracle to His Messenger.

Water was flowing from the tips of his fingers. Grabbing their canteens, everyone rushed to our beloved Prophet's side. They quenched their thirst, they made their ablution, and they watered their animals. Our most beloved Prophet opened his hands, praised and thanked his Lord.

"I bear witness that there is no deity other than Allah and that I am His Messenger," he confirmed.

Meanwhile, the Quraysh were firmly set on not allowing the Messenger of Allah and the believers to enter Mecca. They had no intention of comprehending the fact that the believers had not come to fight. They had come here only to perform their minor pilgrimage. Our Prophet had sent a messenger to clarify the situation, but the non-believers had mistreated him also.

This time, Uthman was going to go to Mecca as messenger. The Messenger of Allah said to him, "Go to the Quraysh and tell them that we are not here for battle. Let them know that we have come only to perform our *umra*. At the same time, invite them to the religion of Islam once more."

Uthman was also going to go and see the believers that had embraced faith but hadn't been able to emigrate to that day and also the ones who had become Muslim in Mecca after the Emigration. He was going to give them the glad tidings of the conquest that was to take place very soon. He was going to announce the wonderful news that soon Allah was going to make His religion dominant over Mecca, and they would no longer have to feel the need to hide themselves. They would soon be able to openly fulfill their religious duties.

Upon arriving in Mecca, without wasting any moment, Uthman started visiting the leaders of the Quraysh. He went to each of them one by one and delivered the message of the Messenger of Allah. However, every one of them exclaimed, "By no means can Muhammad push us around like this!" and closed up their doors completely. On the other hand, to Uthman, they said, "If you want to, you can come and make the *tawaf*, or circumambulation, of the House of Allah." His response was, "I will not circumambulate the House of Allah until the Messenger of Allah is also able to do so," as he rejected their offer.

Uthman had understood the intention of the Quraysh very well. Now, he started knocking on the doors of every believing man and woman in order to fulfill the second duty that our Prophet had given him. The believers were overjoyed when they saw Uthman standing at their door with good news from the Messenger of Allah. As Uthman departed from each of their homes, the believers said, "Send our greetings to the Messenger of Allah," as tears streaked down their faces.

Hudaybiya

Though neither side had any intention to fight, it seemed as though the roads were leading to battle since the sides were unable to come to a mutual understanding. And so, the Quraysh decided to send three messengers to the Messenger of Allah in order to reevaluate the situation; Suhayl ibn Amr, Huwaytib ibn Abdul Uzza, and Mikraz ibn Hafs. The agreement they came to is as follows:

"There isn't a more auspicious deed for us than to come to a peace agreement with Muhammad on the condition that they decide not to make the *tawaf* (circumambulation) of the House of Allah this year and return back to their homes. In this way, those who have heard the news of him and the Arabs coming here will also hear of the way that we have prevented them from entering the city. The following year, they will be able to come again and this time they will be permitted to stay in Mecca for three days and return after they have sacrificed their animals. In this way, they will not have invaded our homeland; instead, they will have spent a few days in the city."

To Suhayl, whom they had chosen as messenger, they said, "Go to Muhammad and come to an agreement with him! But be absolutely sure that the condition of them not entering Mecca this year is in that agreement. We swear to

Allah, we cannot let the Arabs speak later on, here and there, about how they entered our homeland by force."

When Suhayl and his friends reached Hudaybiya, Suhayl immediately went over to our Prophet's side, and they started to talk. After long discussions, they agreed on certain matters and had them written down. The agreement was named after the place they were meeting, Hudaybiya. According to this agreement, they were to not fight among each other throughout a period of ten years. People were to be safe and secure from any possible dangers from either side. Our Prophet and his Companions were going to go back this year, but, the following year, they would be able to visit the House of Allah. In this visit, they would be able to stay in Mecca for three days. Those who were to flee from the Quraysh and seek refuge in our Prophet, without permission from their guardians, were to be returned to their guardian, even if they had accepted Islam as their faith. On the other hand, if one of the Muslims were to take refuge in the Quraysh, they would not be returned. Condemnation and reproach from both sides were to be eradicated, and incidents such as treason and robbery would not be permitted whatsoever. All other tribes and communities aside from the two were free to make agreements and unite with whichever side they pleased at any time they wished.

A new period was going to begin with the Peace Treaty of Hudaybiya. In an environment void of battle, Islam could be spoken of and introduced to many more people in a much more comfortable manner. However, at that moment, the Companions were not yet able to comprehend that aspect of the agreement. Thus, they were not very much pleased with the covenant that had been made. They had come all this way to Hudaybiya with the hopes of performing the tawaf around the Ka'ba, but now they had to leave without fulfilling this dream. For that very moment, the most intense feeling they experienced was disappointment.

First our Prophet, then the Respected Companions performed their sacrifice (of their animal), cut their hair and took off their special dress of consecration. A wind blowing from Hudaybiya carried the strands of their hair towards Mecca.

Finally, after the twenty days they had spent at Hudaybiya, the Muslims started heading back to Medina. As they were travelling on the road, they were commenting on and evaluating the covenant that had just been made. While the majority of the Companions described the covenant as being a great conquest, others preferred to stay silent on the issue. Before long, Surah al-Fath was revealed and brought down by the Archangel Gabriel, and our Prophet conveyed to his Companions that Hudaybiya had, in fact, been a great victory and conquest for the believers. The fact that these happenings were being supported and reinforced through revelation had set the believers' hearts at ease.

The Messengers of Islam

With the Peace Treaty of Hudaybiya, a new period had begun for the Muslims. Speaking about Islam was going to be much easier in this peaceful environment. The most important purpose for a Muslim was to introduce the Almighty Allah to those who don't know Him. However, during the period of fighting and battle, there had not been much opportunity to speak of Islam to greater masses. By means of this new covenant, the safe and secure environment would open the doors to opportunities for people to see the beauties of Islam. The invitation of the Messenger of Allah to the true religion was not particular to only a certain people or a certain land. It was for all of humanity, and the invitation needed to be carried to everyone.

It was the seventh year after Emigration, in the month of Muharram. One day, our Prophet gathered his Companions and said the following, "The Almighty Allah sent me through His Divine Mercy to all of humanity. I ask of you to assist me in announcing the word of Islam to the world! Do not oppose me as his apostles had done to Prophet Jesus, the son of Maryam."

When the Companions asked, "O Messenger of Allah, how had his apostles opposed Prophet Jesus," our Prophet continued, "Just as I want to appoint you with duties in inviting people to Islam, he too had called his apostles to duty. However, his messengers whom he sent to places that were near went willingly whereas the apostles he wished to send further away opposed him and did not want to go. Upon this, Prophet Jesus, upon him be peace, presented the situation to Allah the Almighty and made his complaint. In the morning of that very night, each of the apostles, who had not wanted to go to the faraway lands, came to Prophet Jesus, able to speak the language of the people they were to go to. Jesus, upon him be peace, said to them, 'This is a duty that Allah Himself has certainly appointed you to. Go on now, let all of you go to the places you need to.' Regretful about their previous objections, they set out on the road right away."

Listening very carefully to the Messenger of Allah, the Companions understood very well what he was trying to say to them. As soon as Allah's Messenger finished his words, they responded with one voice, "O Messenger of Allah! We will certainly do anything to help you in this matter. Send us to wherever you wish, we are ready to go!"

Our Prophet was delighted by these words that he heard from his Companions. That day, after the Noon Prayer, he determined the six messengers from his Companions that he would send to other lands with the invitation to Islam. Amr ibn Umayya would go to the Abyssinian king (the Negus) Ashama ibn al-Abjar; Dihya ibn Khalifa al-Kalbi would go to the Byzantine emperor Heraclius; Abdullah ibn Hudhafah as-Sahmi would go to the Persian (Sassanian) king (Khosrau II) Khusraw Parviz; Hatib ibn Abi Balta'ah would go to the Egyptian vicegerent (the Muqawqis) Juraij ibn Matta; Shuja ibn Wahab would go to the king of Damascus, Harith ibn

Abi Shamir al-Ghassan; and Sulayt ibn Amr al-Amiri would go to the chief of Yamama, Hawdha ibn Ali. All of the chosen messengers knew the languages of the lands they would be going to.

After the messengers were appointed, our noble Prophet dictated the letters of invitation to Islam, which would be sent to the rulers of each country. The letters were being prepared. When the Companions drew attention to the fact that the rulers would not read letters that had not been sealed, the Messenger of Allah ordered for a seal to be prepared as well. The seal was carved into a silver ring, and on it was written these words, each one on one line:

Allah

Messenger

Muhammad

After the six letters of invitation were sealed and ready, the Messenger of Allah himself handed the letters to the messengers. Upon receiving the letters, the messengers set out on their journey on that very same day in order to deliver the letters to their rightful destinations.

In this way, the Last Prophet that Allah sent to humanity had announced the religion of Islam to all the rulers and kings of that period, through his messengers. The messengers of Islam faced every possible danger in honor of this cause, and they fulfilled their duties to the best of their ability.

Of the rulers that the messengers reached, some of them accepted this invitation to the truthful religion. Others refused to accept our Prophet as the Last Prophet, though they knew the truth in their hearts. Some did not want to give up their reign. Others tore apart the letter from the Messenger of Allah and threw it on the floor with insolence. And others kissed it, showed it utmost respect and wrapped it in valuable cloths and kept it in precious boxes.

The ones who benefited the most were those who accepted our beloved Prophet's invitation and followed him. And those who not only refused this invitation but behaved disrespectfully and insolently towards the messengers harmed themselves the most.

The Conquest of Khaybar

After the Peace Treaty of Hudaybiya, a kind of tranquili-ty had fallen over the Quraysh. However, the Jews, who had played a big role in igniting the Battle of the Trench by provoking the Quraysh and other Arabian tribes against the Muslims, were not anywhere near at ease. This group, living in Khaybar, was one of the leading powers in the area. Unit-ing with other Jewish groups in the surrounding area, they were planning on a raid into Medina. They still hadn't been able to get over the failure of their plans during the Battle of the Trench, and the desire for revenge was pushing them for-ward. Khaybar was virtually a cauldron of mischief and prov-ocation, and it was boiling to its rim.

The Messenger of Allah had been carefully watching over the developments, and he decided to advance onto Khaybar. The siege in front of the fortresses of Khaybar went on for days with no conclusion. The rain of arrows falling down from the fortress walls started in the early morning hours and continued until nighttime. As the opportunity arose, the believers would fight against the groups that came out of the fortress and the battle would continue until one beat the other.

Finally, one day, the Messenger of Allah turned to his Companions, said, "Tomorrow I will hand over the banner to a man who loves Allah, and Allah loves him," and gave the glad tidings of the conquest of Khaybar.

Nothing was more important for the Companions than to be "the one who loves Allah and the one whom Allah loves." That night, every believer wished that they would be the one to whom the banner would be given. The good news of the conquest that would come the following day had also refreshed and relieved their hearts.

The next morning, after the Morning Prayer, the person to receive the banner from Allah's Messenger was none other than the first of the firsts, Ali.

Handing over the white banner, the Messenger of Allah said to him, "Take this banner and go forward! Keep fighting and do not turn back until the moment that Allah grants you the conquest."

"And for what should I fight the people," asked Ali. Our Prophet replied, "Until they testify that there is no deity but Allah and that Muhammad is His servant and Messenger. Advance until you are in their land and wait for some time; invite them to Islam and let them know of their obligations regarding the rights of Allah and His Messenger. I swear to Allah, for a man to become Muslim through your help is much more blessed than being the owner of valleys filled of red camels!"

The only thing that the Prophet of Compassion wished for these people who had been pouring arrows over them for days was to help them become worthy servants of the Almighty Allah.

Taking the banner of the Messenger of Allah, Ali headed straight for the Khaybar fortresses. The Respected Companions were walking alongside with him. Then he positioned the banner right in front of the fortress. Having been following the happenings from inside the fortress, the Jews were started to grow anxious.

"Who are you," they called out.

"I am the son of Abu Talib, Ali," replied Ali.

This time caused them to panic even more. Hearing the name "Ali," one person started shouting, "O Jewish community! I swear on the book that was revealed to Moses, your end has finally come and you will be defeated!"

It could be understood from this that the writings in their holy book, too, confirmed that it would be Ali who would conquer their fortresses.

As the fortresses were besieged one by one, the people of Khaybar finally understood that they had come to an end, and they submitted. After a period of two months in besiege and a battle afterwards, the problem in Khaybar was finally solved. The Messenger of Allah returned to Medina with his Companions.

The Joy of *Umra* a Year Later

It was the seventh year after the Emigration. The time had come for the believers to perform the *umra*, which they had not been able to the previous year. Our beloved Prophet instructed his Companions to start preparing for the *umra*. Very soon, the dream that the Messenger of Allah had seen a year ago and the glad tidings spoken of in Surah al-Fath would come true. Our Prophet dressed in the special dress of consecration in front of the Masjid an-Nabawi and started chanting the recitations of *talbiya*. All who heard him started reciting along with him. Medina was echoing throughout with the same call: "Labbayk, Allahumma Labbayk; Labbayka la sharika laka labbayk. (Here we are O Allah; here we are at your service! There is no partner with You; here we are!) Inna'l hamda wa'n ni'mata laka wa'l mulka la shariyka lak. (Truly the praise and the provisions are Yours, and so is the dominion and sovereignty. There is no partner with You)."

Two thousand believers headed out of Medina, towards the Ka'ba. Finally they arrived at the Ka'ba. The Messenger of Allah and the Ka'ba were now standing next to each other. The believers and our Prophet performed their duty of *umra* altogether.

The days went by very quickly and the believers, having made the most of the three days they had spent at the Ka'ba in worship, started again back to Medina on their fourth day. During the three days they spent there, the Muslims had said a lot about Islam to the people in Mecca through their disposition and manners. Some liveliness had come to the Ka'ba with the arrival of the believers. People found the opportunity to see the way the Muslims carried out their worship, and small seeds were planted into their hearts in the name of Islam. Immediately following this *umra*, prominent leaders of Mecca such as Khalid ibn Walid, Amr ibn al-As, and Uthman ibn Talha accepted our Prophet and chose the way of Islam. Crushed under the shame of their previous lives, these new believers were full of embarrassment and as they apologized to the Messenger of Allah, his response was crystal clear, "Islam cleanses all previous mistakes before becoming Muslim!"

After such great developments, everyone now saw that the Peace Treaty of Hudaybiya had truly been a conquest. A year ago, they had returned from Hudaybiya without being able to even enter Mecca, and now, just one year later, through Allah's blessing they had been able to enter the people's hearts. From that point on, more and more people started turning to the Messenger of Allah and Islam.

As they went on with their duties of inviting people to Islam and guiding the way of the believers in this environment of peace, something happened to sadden the Messenger of Allah and the believers. Our Prophet had sent Harith to deliver the invitation letter he had written to the governor of Busra. As Harith was passing a place called Balka, the governor of that land, Shurahbil, martyred our Prophet's Companion. This was an inexcusable action because messengers were deemed absolutely untouchable, even under the harshest circumstances. After this incident, it was decided that they do something about this in order to wipe out banditry for good. Because the land they would travel to was under Byzantine rule, the preparations were extensive. As the Islam army of three thousand soldiers headed out, our Prophet asked that they travel to the exact location where his messenger had been martyred and invite the people living there to Islam. As they advanced to their destination, news that the Byzantine had prepared an army of two hundred thousand soldiers reached them. The Muslims were going to face an army which outnumbered them greatly. This battle was named the Battle of Muta. Though the Islam army was very little in number, they showed extraordinary heroism. Khalid had been appointed the commander of the army, and thanks to his very successful battling strategy, the Byzantine army was left with no other choice than to retreat. After hearing the victory of the believers in a battle where there was such a great imbalance of power, every tribe knew for sure that Allah's help and assistance was behind the army of Islam. This was the first blow that hit the Byzantine.

The Covenant is Broken

It was the month of Shaban, in the eighth year after the Emigration. Twenty-two months had passed since the ordering of the Peace Treaty of Hudaybiya. One day, right after the Morning Prayer, some upsetting news from Mecca reached our Prophet. The Qurayshi had organized a midnight raid on the tribe of Huza'a, which had been a tribe protected under the treaty. They were a people who did not harm anyone. They would quietly go on with their lives, and yet a total of twenty-three from among them had been killed. To make matters worse, most of them had been women and children. This was an explicit violation of the Peace Treaty of Hudaybiya.

The leader of the tribe of Huza'a had notified our Prophet of the situation and was asking him for his help.

"Help will be on its way," our Prophet reassured him.

The fact that such an incident had occurred in Mecca, during a period in which they were trying to establish peace throughout the Hijaz made our Prophet very sad. He sent a messenger to the Quraysh asking them to explain the situation. The Quraysh, however, both rejected the fact that they had committed such a deed and also declared that they had abolished the treaty.

Though the Quraysh were speaking is such a bold manner, on the other hand, they were quite anxious, aware of the fact their wrongful actions would cause them trouble. For years they had exposed the Muslims to everything but comfort, but now they had grown fearful of their power. They were neither able to maintain the environment of peace nor did they have the courage to face up to battle. After discussing among themselves, they finally decided to send their leader, Abu Sufyan, to Medina. Though they had intentionally broken the treaty, Abu Sufyan, with intentions of finding reconciliatory ground, was going to speak with the Messenger of Allah, asking him to renew the treaty and extend its time frame. As soon as he reached our Prophet's side, without wasting any time, he got straight to the point, "O Muhammad! I was not present at the Peace Treaty of Hudaybiya. Come now and let us renew the treaty and extend its duration!"

He acted as though he were unaware of the killing in Medina and the violation of the peace treaty. He had brought a whole new issue into question by asking to renew and extend the covenant. The Messenger of Allah wanted to remind him of the previous incident by saying, "Haven't you stirred up an incident beforehand?"

Abu Sufyan replied as though nothing had happened, "We are still bound by the treaty which we signed for at Hudaybiya; we have neither changed nor violated it!" The Messenger of Allah declared, "In actuality, it is us who are still bound by the Peace Treaty of Hudaybiya; we have neither changed nor violated it," in response.

Abu Sufyan continued to repeat the same words over and over. He made no mention whatsoever about their treatment of the people of Huza'a and their violation of peace. Our Prophet was certainly not pleased with such behavior, and without allowing it to continue any longer, he ended this conversation of repeats. That day, Abu Sufyan went to many of the leaders of Medina, including Abu Bakr, Umar, Uthman, Ali and Sa'd ibn Ubadah, speaking to them of the same things also. Unable to reach any conclusion, however, he mounted his camel once again and headed back to Mecca.

A short while after Abu Sufyan's departure, the Messenger of Allah instructed our blessed mother, Aisha, to make preparations for a journey and told her to keep this secret. With help from Allah, the Muslims were going to go to Mecca, but, no matter what, our Prophet did not want any blood to be shed. He wanted to confront the Meccans in a surprising way, without allowing an opportunity for battle to arise. For this reason, they were being extra cautious so as not to let any word escape from Medina to Mecca. Aside from all the precautions they were taking, our beloved Prophet was constantly praying to the Almighty Allah. "O my Gracious Lord! Tie the ears and eyes of the Qurayshi in such a way that they see us in the most unexpected and surprising instant! Let them become aware of our presence only when we have come close to their side and confronted them," he prayed.

On the other hand, messengers were sent in all directions in order to convey the news to all the Muslims: "All that bear faith in Allah and His Messenger shall be prepared and in Medina with the coming of the month of Ramadan!"

With this invitation, the believers arrived in Medina in groups and crowds, one following the other. After some time, all who had become Muslim up to that day were gathered in Medina. In the month of Ramadan of the eighth year after the Emigration, on a Wednesday morning, ten thousand Muslims followed our Prophet and set out on the journey from Medina towards Mecca.

As they reached the valley of Marr ad-Dhahran near Mecca the sky darkened, and it was time for the Night Prayer. They settled there for the night. Then, they all gathered brushwood and twigs and lit a fire on the ground.

On the other side, the Quraysh still had no idea of what was going on. The fact that they hadn't heard anything from Medina after their violation of the peace treaty had made them quite anxious. In the end, they decided to send Abu Sufyan and Hakim ibn Hizam towards Medina in order to gather some news from the surrounding area. They ran across Budayl ibn Warka on the way. He too joined them, and the three of them started heading towards Medina. When they reached Marr ad-Dhahran in the dark of the night, they were shocked. A great army was standing in front of them. As they watched in fear, some of the Companions besieged them from behind. Shortly after, Abu Sufyan and his friends were standing in front of the Messenger of Allah. The leader of Mecca had finally come to the end of an old path and the beginning of a new era. He had been greatly impressed by the strength of our most beloved Prophet and his Companions, their representation of Islam through the language of their disposition, their sincerity and their honorable stand. Flowing through Abu Sufyan's trembling lips were these words: "I bear witness that there is no deity but Allah and I also bear witness that Muhammad is His Messenger!"

Hakim ibn Hizam, who had come along with him on the road, also became a Muslim.

The Conquest of Hearts

It was the 13th of the month of Ramadan and had fallen on a Friday. The army of Islam took off from Marr ad-Dhahran towards Mecca. Our Prophet absolutely did not want any blood to be shed. The only permission to fight was towards those who resisted them. And so, the great conquest had begun. Eight years ago, the Messenger of Allah had left Mecca with only two people, and today, together with those who joined them along the way, they were going to enter the city with twelve thousand. As he advanced along the road, riding his camel Qaswa, he was constantly praising and thanking Allah, reciting the *surah*s, or chapters from the Qur'an, al-Fath and an-Nasr, and was saying, "This is what Allah had promised me."

The city of Mecca had submitted and encompassed into a great silence. They could not stand against the army of Islam with their already scattered army, anyway. There was only one thing that caused the non-believers to worry. All this time, they had committed all the possible evil towards Muhammad, the Trustworthy. They had even attempted to kill him. They wondered, now, what he would do to them.

From that point on, the Messenger of Allah had only one goal, and that was to reunite with the Ka'ba. Our beloved Prophet reached the Ka'ba. As soon as he saw it, he greeted it from afar and then started to shout out cries of *takbir*, or exaltation. His Companions chanted in exaltation together with him. The polytheists had run to the tops of the surrounding mountains, and, with alarm, they listened to the shouts of praise which filled the earth and skies. After circling around the Ka'ba in worship, the Ka'ba was thoroughly cleansed of the idols and pictures, atop, inside and out.

Meanwhile, the time for the Noon Prayer had come. Upon the request of our Prophet, Bilal stood atop the Ka'ba and cried out the call for the Noon Prayer. This holy structure was finally freed of being the center for idolatry and had once again reached its true identity.

Meanwhile, the people were standing in the courtyard of the Ka'ba and were waiting to hear our Prophet's decision about what was to become of them. Starting his words with words of praise to Allah, the Messenger of Allah said, "O people of Quraysh! How do you expect me to judge you on this day?"

These people had harmed both our beloved Prophet and the believers in every possible way, and so deserved every kind of punishment. However, the Prophet of mercy and compassion was going to approach them in a most different way. He forgave all those people who had done nothing but evil and harm for all these years. After all, he had been sent for the salvation of all humankind. When met with such great compassion, the Meccan polytheists could not help but say, "You truly must be the Prophet of Allah. Such goodness and compassion can only be found in a Prophet of Allah. You are, after all, known among us for your benevolence and trustworthiness." After all the things that they heard and experienced on that day, their hearts truly softened and, group by group, they accepted the religion of Islam as their faith. Praising his Gracious Lord for this conquest of hearts, the Messenger of Allah provided lengthy information to the believers, who had been honored with the religion of Islam on that day, about their newly chosen religion. For days, afterwards, it was as though the Meccan Muslims were racing with each other in this conquest.

Now, our Prophet's intention was to go back to Medina. However, news coming from the polytheist tribes surrounding Mecca was not very pleasant. After hearing of the conquest of Mecca, the Hawazin and Thaqif tribes had grown anxious about their own fates. They said, "Now, it will be our turn. We must confront them before they have a chance to confront us," and tried to gather more and more people to support them. Paying heed to this news they confronted the affiliate army of polytheists and defeated them. This battle was called the Battle of Hunayn. Following the battle, some leaders of the tribes ran off to Ta'if and took refuge there. Their intention was to gather strength there and prepare to attack the Muslims once more. And, indeed, the people of Ta'if united and did so.

After hearing of the recent developments, the new target for the believers was Ta'if. First of all, the Messenger of Allah sent a vanguard troop to Ta'if, under the leadership of Khalid ibn Walid. Khalid made great effort to discuss and come to an agreement with the people of Ta'if, but when they openly challenged the Muslims in response, the Messenger of Allah also changed his direction towards Ta'if. Ta'if was a city full of bitter memories for our Prophet. Ten years ago, he had arrived in this city wanting to invite its people to Islam and the message from Allah and had left wounded and bleeding. Ta'if was still the same Ta'if. Despite all the years that had passed and all the beautiful things that had occurred in the name of faith, they still insisted on denying the truth. As they drew closer to Ta'if they offered to sit and discuss once more, but the people of Ta'if responded with arrows, stones and catapults. Then the siege began. More than twenty days passed without being able to come to any positive conclusion. The Messenger of Allah ordered for the siege to be lifted and the Islam army started to leave Ta'if. As they headed back, the Messenger of Allah turned towards the fortresses of Ta'if, opened his hands to the skies and prayed, "O my Gracious Lord! Guide the people of Thaqif to the truthful path, relieve them of their financial difficulties and enable them to join us in belief."

A Center of Trust and Security

After a long separation, the Messenger of Allah was back in Medina once again. It was the beginning of a brand-new period in Medina. People travelled to Medina in groups, coming to visit our Prophet, accepting the religion of Islam and becoming honored with the blessing of faith. Medina, a city which had been torn apart by war until recently, had surpassed its previous state in only a matter of nine years. It was now a center which distributed trust and security to the rest of the world. Throughout the years following the emigration to Medina, Allah had glorified the religion of Islam. Everything else besides the true religion was now deemed lowly and worthless.

However, there were some groups who were not pleased with these positive developments. One of them happened to be among the most powerful empires of the time, the Byzantine. Ever since the Battle of Muta, the Byzantine King Heraclius had been having the intention to invade the Arabian Peninsula in order to put an end to the spread of Islam. With the support of the Christian Arabs and certain other tribes, Heraclius had gathered a great army and was prepared to confront Medina. As soon as our Prophet grew aware of the situation, he ordered his Companions to prepare for battle. During the preparations, the respected Companions of our Prophet showed great selflessness as they sacrificed whatever they possessed, in the way of Allah. The Islam army came all the way to Tabuk, but the Byzantine were nowhere to be seen. Fearing that he would lose his throne, the King Heraclius had retreated. Thus, the strength and durability of the Byzantine had fallen, and the news spread throughout the land. After consultation among each other, the Messenger of Allah and his respected Companions decided to depart from Tabuk. They headed back to Medina all together.

Together with our Prophet's return from Tabuk came the acceleration of the groups of people flocking into Medina. Medina was now hosting a new group of guests almost every single day. The success of the Muslims in very important turning points, such as the Conquest of Mecca and the battles of Hunayn and Tabuk, had paved the way for people's hearts to open up to Islam. In only a year, Medina hosted nearly three hundred fifty different groups, each consisting of a different number of people. Most of them returned to their own tribes after becoming Muslim. The excitement of those returning home after being honored with Islam was matchless. They were practically running back to their homes to introduce Islam to their own family and close ones. The people of Thaqif had stood against our Prophet during the siege of Ta'if in the eighth year of the Hijra. In the ninth year of the Hijra, following the expedition to Tabuk, the same people sent a group from among them to become Muslim.

As more and more people came to Medina, the Messenger of Allah sent some of his Companions to different places in order to teach people about Islam, at the same time. These individuals invited the people there to Islam, taught them the essentials of the religion and also represented the beauty of Islam through their lifestyles.

The First and Last Pilgrimage

It was the ninth year of Emigration. The verse, "Pilgrimage to the House of Allah is a duty owed to Allah by all who can afford a way to it," was revealed in the month of Dhu al-Qadah. Through this verse Hajj, or pilgrimage, had become an obligatory act of worship. When they reached the month of Dhu al-Qadah of the tenth year, our Prophet announced to his Companions that he was going to go to Mecca, in order to fulfill his duty of Pilgrimage. Upon this, Muslims from all around started flocking into Medina so that they too could perform their Pilgrimage together with our most beloved Prophet.

After all preparations had been completed, five days before the month of Dhu al-Qadah finished, on a Saturday afternoon, the Muslims set out from Medina after they had performed the Noon Prayer. When they reached a place called Dhu'l-Hulayfa, the Messenger of Allah cleansed himself through ablution of his whole body, put on nice fragrances, and dressed in his special garment of consecration. He announced to his Companions that they were to make their intentions for both the Pilgrimage and the *umra*. Before heading out on the journey, he had informed his Companions about the many different aspects relating to their Pilgrimage. Our Prophet had also brought with him approximately one hundred camels as their sacrificial animals. The Messenger of Allah headed forward while chanting the recitations of *talbiya*. His Companions joined him and as the believers cried out,

"Labbayk Allahumma Labbayk. Labbayka la sharika laka labbayk. Inna'l hamda wa'n ni'mata laka wa'l mulka la shariyka lak," they headed towards Mecca.

They followed the path they had used during the Emigration, and by the fourth day of Dhu al-Hijjah they had arrived in Mecca. Without any delay, our Prophet headed towards the Ka'ba, greeted the Rukn, and started to make the tawaf afterwards. As soon as he completed his tawaf, circling around the Ka'ba, he performed a two-*rakah* Prayer between the Ka'ba and the Sacred Station of Prophet Ibrahim. During this Prayer, he recited Surah al-Kafirun and al-Ikhlas. Then he came back to the Rukn, greeted it, and turned towards Safa. He completed the *sa'y* between the hills of Safa and Marwa, climbed atop the hill of Safa and after turning towards the Ka'ba and shouting out cries of exaltation, he raised his hands and prayed.

Starting from a Sunday, the Messenger of Allah spent four days in Mecca. On the eighth day of Dhu al-Hijjah he headed towards Mina, together with his Companions. A tent was put up for him in a place called Namira, and, there, our Prophet performed his five Daily Prayers.

On the ninth day of Dhu al-Hijjah, the day of Arafa, they came to the place called Arafat. In the middle of the valley of Arafat, in the afternoon, atop his camel Qaswa, the Messenger of Allah delivered his Farewell Sermon to the one hundred twenty thousand Companions surrounding him. In this sermon, he gave his last pieces of advice concerning the true religion of Islam. At the end of the sermon, he said, "O humankind! Tomorrow, they will ask you of me. What will you say then?" The Muslims replied, "You preached the Allah's religion. You fulfilled your duty. We bear witness to this."

Upon hearing this, our Prophet raised his blessed index finger, then turned it onto his community, and released it, saying, "Witness this O my Lord! Witness this O my Lord! Witness this O my Lord!"

Later on, our Prophet performed the *waqfa*, standing there facing the *qiblah*, until sundown. Following Muzdalifah and Mina, the sacrificing of the animals was carried out. After the Messenger of Allah completed the farewell tawaf, they headed back to Medina. This pilgrimage, in which Allah's Messenger bid farewell to his Companions, was the first and the last pilgrimage that our Prophet would perform. The thousands of Muslims who had come with him on this Pilgrimage also went back to where they had come from and continued to live by and spread the one and true religion, Islam.

Time for the Farewell

The day our Prophet delivered his Farewell Sermon, the third verse of Surah al-Maedah was also revealed. It read, "This day I have perfected for you your Religion (with all its rules, commandments and universality), completed My favor upon you, and have been pleased to assign for you Islam as religion. "Upon hearing this verse, some of the Companions understood that this was a kind of sign indicating that the decease of the Messenger of Allah was drawing near, and they cried. Indeed, in very little time, our most beloved Prophet would reunite with his Lord. The Last Prophet, who had been sent as a mercy to all the worlds, was now sixty-three years old. Inflicted with fever, the Messenger of Allah was lying in his bed, burning from high fever. With each day, his illness grew even stronger. In the first couple of days that he had fallen sick, at times when his fever died down, he was able to come to the masjid and lead his Companions in Prayer. One day, when his illness was not so intense, he came to the masjid, stood up on the pulpit, and called out to his Companions,

"O my Companions, no Prophet has ever lived within his community for eternity. Know that one day I, too, will reunite with my Lord. Surely, you, too, will reunite with your Lord one day.

The earth shall be left to no one. Every single thing is dependent on the will of Allah. It is not possible to either draw closer or avoid the time that Allah has appointed for us. The place in which we will all meet is by the Pool of Al-Kawthar (Abundant Goodness). Whoever wishes to meet with me by the side of the Pool of Al-Kawthar should protect their hand and tongue and keep them away from evil deeds. O my Companions! Allah has given freedom to one of His servants, to choose between the worldly life and the life of the Hereafter. And this servant has chosen the life of the Hereafter."

As these words flowed through his blessed lips, Abu Bakr started to cry. He had understood that through these words, the Messenger of Allah was giving them the message of his decease.

Our Prophet reassured him, saying, "Do not cry O Abu Bakr." Then he said,

"In my eyes, Abu Bakr is the most trustworthy and strong of human beings in terms of his physical and spiritual devotion and selflessness. If I were to choose a bosom friend other than my Lord, I would certainly choose Abu Bakr as my friend. However, from now on, there is only the brotherhood of Islam and the love that is centered around this brotherhood. Even if all doors opening to the Masjid are closed, leave Abu Bakr's door open!"

It was as though the Messenger of Allah was bidding farewell with his every word. The Companions were all very downhearted and unhappy, and no one could hold back their tears any more.

It was the Thursday before the decease of the Messenger of Allah. His illness had become much more intense by now.

There were times when he lost consciousness and fainted. He had fainted once again while the congregation was waiting for him to join them in performing the Night Prayer. As soon as he woke up he asked our blessed mother Aisha whether they had prayed or not. Aisha told him that the congregation was waiting for him, and he asked her to prepare water so that he could make his ablution. However, just as he was about to go out to the *masjid* for the Prayer, he fainted once again. When he woke up he asked about the Prayer again. He wanted to lead the Prayer, but he was constantly fainting and coming back. Thereupon, he asked that Abu Bakr lead the Prayer. He, himself, came out to pray with the help of two of his Companions. When the congregation saw him, they grew very excited. When Abu Bakr took a step back so that our Prophet could lead the Prayer, the Messenger of Allah signaled for him to stay where he was. With help, he came up to Abu Bakr's side. Because he had no strength to stand, he completed his Prayer while sitting down.

From that day on, the Messenger of Allah appointed Abu Bakr to lead the Prayers in his place. Still, every day, the Respected Companions waited for him with hope.

They had come to a Monday now. The Monday that fell on the 12th day of the month of Rabi al-Awwal... The Companions had filled the masjid for the Morning Prayer. The leader of the congregation was Abu Bakr once again. For an instant, there was a kind of activity in the masjid. The Messenger of Allah had come to the Masjid an-Nabawi. The Companions were just about to end their Prayer because of their joy. They had stood up for the second *rakah* of the Prayer when the Messenger of Allah arrived right behind Abu Bakr. When

Abu Bakr wanted to take a step back, our Prophet touched his shoulder, wanting him to stay there, and he joined in the Prayer from where he sat behind him. After the leader turned and completed the Prayer, our Prophet continued and finished the *rakah* which he hadn't been able to catch up to. This had been our Prophet's last Prayer. As he left the masjid, he turned to his Companions and said, "A Prophet does not die until one of his Companions leads him in Prayer." With that he returned to his room.

Sometime later, the sun had risen and it was nearly mid-morning. The Messenger of Allah was giving advice to those around him, telling them to work for their afterlife while they still had the chance. Meanwhile, he turned to Fatima, who was crying and shedding tears by her blessed father's bed side, and said, "My daughter, you must be patient for a while. You must not cry. For the Archangels in the heavens cry when they see you crying."

He wiped away Fatima's tears, consoled her, and prayed for Allah the Almighty to give her forbearance. Then he said, "O my daughter, every misfortune receives its compliment. From now on, there shall be no sorrow or pain for your father."

He took his grandsons, Hasan and Husayn, by his side, looked at them with compassion and kissed them on their foreheads. A short while later, our Prophet's condition started changing. At that moment, the Archangel Gabriel had come and brought news from his Lord.

"You Lord says," he said, "If he wishes, I will heal him and make him better, but if he wishes, I will take him to My presence and embrace him with My Mercy!"

Our beloved Prophet's response to the Archangel of revelation was, "This is a task which belongs to my Lord. He will do as He wished for me." Then the Archangel Gabriel said,

"O Messenger of Allah! The Archangel of Death is waiting at your door. He is asking for permission to enter. He has never asked for permission from anyone before. And he will not ask anyone else after this."

Allah's Messenger gave permission and the Archangel Azrael, upon him be peace, entered. He greeted our beloved Prophet and said, "O Messenger of Allah! The Almighty Allah has sent me to your presence. He commanded me to obey your orders. If you wish so, let me take your honorable soul and lift it to the Sublime Realm, and if not, then I shall return and leave."

The Messenger of Allah replied, "O Archangel Azrael, fulfill your duty."

Meanwhile, he stroke his blessed face with his dampened hands and said, "O my Gracious Lord! Help me in overcoming the hardship of death!"

He rested his blessed head on Aisha's bosom and fixed his black eyes on the ceiling. All the while, he was uttering, "*La ilaha illallah* (There is no deity but Allah)! Truly, there is serious stupor in death." He had fainted again. A while later, he came back to himself.

Meanwhile, his finger was pointing to the skies. His eyes were directed to the ceiling once again, and his lips were moving. Our blessed mother Aisha hear him uttering these words, "Please forgive and embrace me with Your Mercy, together with the Prophets, the martyrs and the true believers upon whom You bestowed blessings. Accept me to Your highest Companionship! O my Gracious Lord, I wish for You as a Glorious Friend! O my Gracious Lord, I wish for You as a Glorious Friend! O my Gracious Lord, I wish for You as a Glorious Friend!"

This blessed life had started sixty-three years ago, on a Monday, and now it was coming to an end, once again on a Monday. Our blessed Prophet entrusted those after him with the blessed duty of conveying Allah's message. He was finally able to rejoice in reuniting with his Lord and the Most Beloved.

After the decease of our Prophet, the Muslims went through indescribable grief and shed many tears after him. It was with him that they had seen and learned about everything there was. The world, the Hereafter, the gardens of Paradise, the pits of Hell, hope... It was thanks to him that they were saved from complete perish and abandonment. It was through him that they learned to wish for eternity and not fear death; it was through him that they came to know the Lord of the Worlds. They had been blessed with the honor of spending years by his side, becoming his Respected Companions.

We have never seen him but have lived on with his memories, with him in our dreams. It was he, the beloved Last Prophet, who said, "My brothers will come in the End Times," and we seek to be of those he calls, "My brothers!" May Allah the Almighty grant us with the blessing of never faltering from the path of our most beloved Prophet in this world and grant us the honor of being with him in the gardens of Paradise.

We are indebted to you and all our gratefulness is upon you. May your intercession be upon us, our beloved Prophet!

Sources

Burak, Bekir, *Hazreti Hatice*, İstanbul: Rehber Yayınları, 2005.

Burak, Bekir, *Hazreti Ebû Bekir*, İstanbul: Rehber Yayınları, 2005.

Burak, Bekir, *Hazreti Ali*, İstanbul: Rehber Yayınları, 2005.

Canan, İbrahim, *Kütüb-i Sitte*, Ankara: Akçağ Yayınları, 1992.

Haylamaz, Reşit, *Gönül Tahtımızın Eşsiz Sultanı Efendimiz 1–2*, İstanbul: Işık Yayınları, 2006.

Haylamaz, Reşit, *Dillerdeki Müjde*, İstanbul: Işık Yayınları, 2005.

Haylamaz, Reşit, *Saadet Asrına Doğan İlk Yıldızlar*, İstanbul: Işık Yayınları, 2005.

Kandehlevî, M. Yusuf, *Hayâtü's Sahabe*, Semerkand Yayıncılık, 2003.

Köksal, M. Asım, *İslâm Tarihi*, Şâmil Yayınevi, 1987.

Suruç, Salih, *Kâinatın Efendisi Peygamberimizin Hayatı*, İstanbul: Nesil Yayınları, 2007.